STREEP

A Life in Film

Also by Iain Johnstone

Non-fiction

The Arnhem Report

Dustin Hoffman

The Man With No Name

The Bond Companion

Tramp's Gold

Richard By Kathryn

Tom Cruise: All The World's A Stage

Fiction

Cannes; The Novel

Wimbledon 2000

Fierce Creatures (With John Cleese)

Pirates Of The Mediterranean

STREEP

A Life in Film

Iain Johnstone

Psychology News Press
London

dcpsychologynews@googlemail.com

Cover: Ian Hughes

Set in Palatino
by Keyboard Services, Luton
keyboardserv@sky.com

Printed and bound in the UK by
CPI Mackays, Chatham ME5 8TD

Distributed by Melia Publishing Services
Godalming
Telephone 01483 869839
melia@melia.co.uk

ISBN 978–0–907633–20–4
ISBN Paperback 978-0-907633-80-8

Contents

For Holly

'Meryl's got to be one of those phenomena, like Garbo, that happens once in a generation.'

Mike Nichols

'She plays all of us better than we play ourselves.'

Nora Ephron, director *Sleepless in Seattle*

'She could play the Brooklyn Bridge – and make us believe it.'

Robert Redford

'I just wanted to get a job in a nice regional theatre and meet a fella.'

Meryl Streep, 2008

The Family

Meryl Streep, born 1949

Don Gummer, born 1952

Children:

Henry, born 1979

Mamie, born 1983

Grace, born 1986

Louisa, born 1991

Preface

Every biography is a journey; the destination can be very different from the point of departure. I have interviewed Meryl Streep on four occasions – in a televised Guardian Lecture at The National Film Theatre, for a BBC profile of her on location with *Plenty* and twice for *The Sunday Times* – and, obviously, on each occasion I researched her life and work. But the result of writing this book has revealed, to me at least, a woman who is more insightful and instinctive about the ways of the cinema than anyone I've ever met. She is also much funnier but, at the same time, ruthlessly determined and virtually out of sight of her peer group in terms of her achievements.

I haven't gone through every one of her nearly 60 films (for that there is a filmography at the end of the book) but, in a personal fashion, I have tried to find lines through her career in terms of time and genres ('tragical-comical-historical', as Polonius said to the Players, plus, maybe, post-modernist – and musical!)

It is impossible to quantify talent, but the fact that she has been nominated for more Academy Awards

(15) and Golden Globes (23) than any other actor in film history suggests that there are others out there who agree she is rather good. Fifteen Oscar nominations in a 32-year film career lead one to suspect that maybe somewhere in the Academy Members Handbook there is a rule which insists that Meryl Streep *must* be nominated every two years at least.

At the same time Streep has managed to sustain a marriage to the sculptor, Don Gummer, for more than 30 years and she has brought up four children very much in private. Readers who are hoping for scandal, sex, drugs and rock and roll are likely to be disappointed. Readers who want to learn about acting, how to choose parts, or the politics of Hollywood will not be.

Meryl Streep and Don Gummer live in Connecticut and Manhattan and have a son and three daughters: Henry who was born in 1979, Mamie who was born in 1983, Grace who was born in 1986, and Louisa who was born in 1991.

Streep has made it a policy of leading as normal a private life as possible. If you report on films as I have done, you get used to the number of security guards who accompany stars such as Tom Cruise or Brad Pitt and Angelina Jolie wherever they go, but Streep will have none of this. When her son Henry was at Glasgow University, she frequently visited him, staying on her own at the small, discreet but very stylish hotel, One Devonshire Gardens. When she went to local supermarkets to buy him food and other student necessities, people 'thought' they recognised her but, as she said, 'they tended to think it was just someone who looked like me because they didn't expect to see the real me there.'

22nd June 2009 is Streep's 60th birthday. We are supposed to slow down as we get older but the remarkable thing is that her work in this last decade has, in its infinite variety, been exceptional. The range runs from the outrageous, over-the-top fashionista fascista in *The Devil Wears Prada* (2006) to the soft-spoken CIA officer who authorises torture in *Rendition* (2006), from the hippy dancing queen in *Mamma Mia!* (2008) to the nasty nun in *Doubt*, both shot in the same year.

Streep once told me that she feared the fate of Katharine Hepburn, who had won her first Oscar for *Morning Glory* (1933) at an age when Streep hadn't even stepped in front of a camera. But then, from 1935, Hepburn appeared in a succession of flops and was deemed 'box-office poison' by The Independent Theatre Owners of America.

Streep was nominated for an Oscar for her second film, *The Deer Hunter* (1978), and was fearful the curse of Kate might descend on her. So she signed up for four more films immediately. But there was no need to panic: the fourth, *Kramer vs. Kramer* (1979) landed her an Oscar and her stellar cinema career was assured. She had no need to play the Hepburn card. A despondent Hepburn had left California and returned to Broadway to act in *The Philadelphia Story*. But, with her impresario instinct, she took no money for acting in it but asked for the film rights instead. Hepburn then returned to Hollywood and added Cary Grant and Jimmy Stewart, like salt and pepper, and the rest is history. Nine films with Spencer Tracy made her a grand dame who starred in films for another 40 years.

As actresses they are considerably different; Hepburn

seldom dropped her Bryn Mawr accent while Streep has seldom used the same one twice. Although Streep looked up to Hepburn, the admiration was not reciprocated. Hepburn maintained that she could see Streep actively searching for tactics and ploys in the middle of performing – she could hear the wheels turning in her head. When her official biographer, A. Scott Berg, asked her what she thought of Streep, Hepburn in grande bitch mode simply answered, 'Click, click, click.' Berg later said that if she had seen Streep's comedies she would have changed her mind but the truth was she could easily have seen them, since she died in June 2003, years after Streep had given lessons in crisp and immaculate timing in *Postcards from the Edge* (1990) and *Death Becomes Her* (1992).

Unlike Hepburn, Streep has neither had the inclination nor the need to initiate movie properties; scripts have come to her like antelopes to a water hole. As an actor, this meant she could clear her mind to prepare her performance and make it as near perfect as possible. For instance, to play the part of Sophie Zawistowski – the Polish girl who survives Auschwitz and comes to New York – in *Sophie's Choice* (1982), Streep took the trouble to learn Polish, a notoriously difficult language. Few, if any, other actors would go to such trouble. The character speaks English – as well as she can – in the film but Streep wanted her to *think* in Polish and let her diction and expression come from that. Not only does Polish put adjectives before or after nouns depending on the circumstances of the sentence, but in spoken Polish, the stress falls on the penultimate syllable of any given word. Not many people will have spotted that subtlety the first time they saw Streep's performance – or in subsequent viewings, come to that.

Is it possible to work out why Streep, virtually alone among her contemporaries, has been so durable? There is one seminal clue and it lies in her education. Malcolm Gladwell in his book *Outliers* – an outlier is 'a statistical observation that is markedly different from the others of the sample' – tries to prove that it isn't just pure talent that takes certain people to the very top. He quotes the neurologist, Daniel Levitin, who, from scientific experiments, concluded that added to the talent there has to be at least 10,000 hours of practice. The evidence is plausible in the case of The Beatles who, before they sprung fully-formed on an unsuspecting world, had performed more than twelve hundred times in eight hour gigs during five trips to Hamburg – more hours, Gladwell observes, than most bands play in their entire careers.

Gladwell's equations don't work so well with Mozart. He claims that the young genius didn't compose anything of great merit until his piano concertos of 1777 when he was 21. Those of us who rate the composer's 'Exsultate, Jubilate', K. 165, which he wrote when he was only 17, would beg to differ.

But what if Gladwell were to apply his arithmetic to Meryl Streep? She spent seven years in university education, four at Vassar and a further three at Yale Drama School. Let us suppose those 21 terms were ten weeks each. We reach 210. And let us suppose she tended to work six days a week – that's 1,260 days. At eight hours a day. The total comes to, yes, 10,800 hours. Even perhaps more significantly, during that time Streep acted in more than 40 amateur productions before she received a single dollar for stepping onto the professional stage. She was not under-prepared.

Hollywood today is a very different place from the town in which Irving Thalberg or David O. Selznick could trust their instincts and churn out one profitable picture after another. They were helped by a virtually captive audience. Sixty years ago, 90 million Americans went to a movie every week – out of a population of only 150 million. Nowadays nervous studios each back fewer than 20 films a year and, fearing the new, seek safety in sequels. In 2008 Universal released *Hellboy 2*, *Mummy 3* and *Indiana Jones 4*. Although *Mamma Mia!* was to take $580 million on screens throughout the world, the studio budgeted it at a cautious $50m.

The proportion of flops to hits throughout the studios is something over 5 to 1 with the latter compensating for the former. The writer William Goldman's observation 'Nobody knows anything' is much parroted in any analysis of the film industry but there is always the exception that proves the rule – the exception is Meryl Streep does.

In an industry obsessed by special effects movies, comic book movies, gangster movies, science fiction movies and pirate pictures, she has threaded a steady course through this maelstrom with a choice of material that is – for the most part – clever, well written and inevitably, well performed. Her success-rate is better than one in two.

Why should that be? I have met, worked with and interviewed many people in the film industry – including various studio chiefs and their successors – over the past 40 years and have never encountered anybody with a mind as acute or as intuitive a nose for a quality film as she has.

After her three years at Yale Drama School, Streep worked at New York's Public Theatre under Joe Papp and, later, on Broadway. Her cumulative experience meant that Streep had learned virtually everything there was to know about performance, script, direction, casting and, most important of all, audiences. How could anybody who had taken the traditional route from the post room of a Hollywood talent agency to be head of a studio have a pedigree that was in any way a match for that?

Now that she is nearly 60, is Streep going to slow down or, even, stop? She could live a contented home life all year long in Salisbury, Connecticut, attending to her charities, to her husband Don and to her children. In her time off from making movies she already does. The owner of the local store watches her arrive in her eco-friendly car, stock up with groceries and good wine for the week-end and pay for them with a cheque signed, significantly, 'Mary Louise Gummer'. Psychologists might say that she is trying to maintain some distance between the housewife and the star.

Streep will qualify for free Dial-a-Ride from Salisbury town council, she can gain entry to Dodd Stadium to watch the Defenders baseball team for $3 on Wednesday afternoons and can get into the State Fair for free and observe the judging of – or even judge – the Quilt Contest.

All this is possible. But improbable. Streep already has her performance as cookery writer Julia Child in Nora Ephron's *Julie and Julia* in the can – a project they held back not just so there wasn't a log-jam of Streep nominations at the 2008 awards ceremonies but also because, based on the hit openings of *The Devil Wears Prada* and *Mamma Mia!* in the States, the studios now believe there is a 'Streep Slot' when her movies will earn most effectively at the box office – shortly after Independence Day (4th July).

Then Nancy Myers, who wrote *Private Benjamin* and *Father of the Bride*, is pairing her with Steve Martin and Alec Baldwin in a love triangle rom-com, due for release on Christmas Day 2009. And then, after that, she is likely to be the librarian watching the pussy come in through the book-return slot in Vicki Myron's *Dewey: The Small-Town Library Cat Who Touched the World*.

And then … and then … and on … and on.

Why *should* she stop? Katharine Hepburn shot three films in the year she turned 84. Estelle Winwood, a star schooled at Liverpool Rep, appeared in the coroner series *Quincy M.E.* when she was 97. And, no, she didn't play the corpse.

So this is but a half-term report on a life in films. I hope to give the reader some insight into what makes Streep Streep and, for students of drama, film and the media, an inside look at what it takes to get to the top – and stay there.

1

Starring at Yale

Meryl Streep's DNA is a mini European Union in its own right. Her father's ancestors were originally called Messerschmitz. They were Spanish Sephardic Jews who moved to Holland and married there. When they converted to Christianity, they decided to change their name. There is a Dutch saying, 'zet er een streep onder' which means 'let's start over again' with 'streep' meaning 'line' as in 'dividing line'. So Streep they became. Her mother's ancestors were English, Irish and Swiss.

Mary Louise Streep was born in Summit, New Jersey on 22nd June 1949. Her father, Harry Streep II, was in the marketing department of the pharmaceutical giant, Merck. Her mother, Mary, was a freelance commercial artist. She was 35 when she gave birth to Mary Louise and soon gave her two baby brothers for company: Dana, and Harry III.

It was a musical family with father playing the piano and Mary an accomplished singer. 'They fell in love over the piano. My father loved to play the piano and I remember my mother singing in the kitchen – that's how we knew she was mad' Streep laughs. 'I heard every single song from the '30s and '40s. She knew the lyrics to everything.' Later Harry lll became a dancer and choreographer.

Summit – so-called because in 1837 the railroad tracks were laid over Summit Hill in the Watchung Reservation – was bought from the native Americans in 1664. As usual the redskins got skinned and traded land for two coats, two kettles, two guns and twenty handfuls of powder. Over time it became a typical middle-class, family-orientated community, within easy reach of New York but with the benefit of clear mountain air.

The Streeps were an upwardly-mobile family, adding to their status with every move they made to larger houses in the district. Usually granny came too, and the first hints of Streep's talents surfaced early in life when she did imitations of the elderly lady, borrowing her cardigan and drawing lines on her own face to age it. At home she would dragoon her younger brothers into making films with their father's ciné camera; at school she made an early mark singing 'Holy Night' in a Christmas production. Not only was she note-perfect but word-perfect as well – in flawless French.

Behind so many major success stories there is a forceful parent and Mary Streep certainly was that. Every week she would drive her daughter to Manhattan for singing lessons with Estelle Liebling, once John Philip Sousa's favourite soprano. As a teacher she was still a force to be reckoned with, even in her eighties: one of Streep's fellow pupils was Beverly Sills, then in her prime and training her voice to sing Cleopatra in

Handel's *Julius Caesar* at the opening of the new Metropolitan Opera House at Lincoln Center. You don't have to be Precious Ramotswe of the Number One Ladies' Detective Agency to conclude that it was Mary Streep's passionate desire that her daughter become a Diva.

Trips to Manhattan inevitably included a theatre matinée so, before she became a teenager, there were strong hints of the direction Streep's career might take. When, in later life, she was asked who her greatest influence had been, she said that person was her 'greatest producer', her mother.

She gave her mother praise most parents can only dream of; Streep had no problem saying it while Mary was alive and could appreciate it:

'My mother was and is my role model. Not precisely for what she did in her life, but for the way she's always done everything. She always started the day singing, she loves a good joke, she has energy and verve, wit and great natural graciousness. Everybody loves my mom because she is the Will Rogers of women; she puts people at their ease and can diffuse any awkward social situation with a witty aside or a joke at her own expense. I've always admired this ability to lighten the atmosphere when she enters the room, and I think the best role models for women and girls are people of either gender who are fruitfully and confidently themselves, who bring light into the world.'

We seldom have the same view of ourselves that others have. At Bernardsville High School, Streep considered herself something of an outsider, rather geeky in her round spectacles, and not over-confident. To most of her contemporaries, however, she was a star. When she was 15 she got the lead, Marian, the librarian, in Meredith Wilson's *The Music Man*. One day, during rehearsal, her English master was walking past the window of the rehearsal room. He could hear a woman's voice singing ''Til There Was You' so consummately that he assumed the drama teacher must have brought some professionals into the cast. When he entered the room he was, to say the least, surprised to see the singer was the little bespectacled girl who sat next to the wall in his English class.

Streep got a standing ovation from the audience every night, something, she claims, that has never happened to her since. Her drama teacher, Dick Everhart, observed: 'When she walked out on the stage, there was nobody else there.' Streep herself says: 'If I can locate the moment when I was first bitten, that was it.'

Streep exchanged her spectacles for contact lenses, dyed her hair blonde and out went the lack of confidence and in came the champion swimmer, the Cheerleader and the Homecoming Queen. Homecoming Queen?

The ceremony of Homecoming was dreamt up in 1910 at the University of Illinois. Two students thought it would be good to bring back the alumni from previous years for a game of football, a dance or the inevitable parade or, preferably, all three. The idea spread to high schools, and the two students who had done most for the school were elected Homecoming King and Queen to preside over the events of the day. The vote was, in effect, a popularity contest and certainly confirmed Streep's status at Bernardsville High.

As a striking blonde cheerleader Streep had her pick of the football team and her favours fell on a working-class hunk, Bruce Thomson. 'My favourite part of high school was the boys who sat in the back row – they were so funny,' she later recalled. 'So much of what I know about comedy – even the most sophisticated comedy – comes from high school because it's such a painful, funny time. And some of the boys in the back row, who now sell real estate in New Jersey, were the most brilliantly funny people in the whole world. I was a very good audience before I ever thought of being a performer.'

It was unlikely that Streep would ever end up selling real estate, or in any other humdrum job. She had a first-class academic mind and won a scholarship to Vassar to study English and Drama in September 1967. The college has its picturesque campus on the outskirts of Poughkeepsie in the Hudson Valley. One can imagine Streep dressed, according to one contemporary, in an old felt hat, a black turtle-neck sweater and boots, devouring everything from Jane Austen to James Baldwin. Weekday life for the two thousand or so young ladies there was not disrupted by men – Vassar students would go by bus to Yale at the weekends to remind themselves the other gender did exist. But in Streep's third year, the college became mixed – one of the few Seven Sisters' universities to make such a change.

Streep seems to have had a very contented life there, singing with the 'Night Owls', being elected vice-president of her class in her sophomore year and, according to a former roommate, owning 'the biggest collection of Johnny Mathis records in the world.'

When not following the love life of Mr Darcy to the strains of 'Misty', Streep devoted herself to her main consuming passion: theatre. Her drama teacher, Clinton Atkinson, asked her to read a passage from *A Streetcar Named Desire* in which Blanche DuBois is taken to the hospital after suffering a frightening nervous breakdown. 'Her acting was hair-raising, absolutely mind-boggling,' he recalled later. 'I don't think anyone ever taught Meryl acting, she really taught herself.'

Streep had actually never acted in a drama until her second year at university, when she won the title role in August Strindberg's *Miss Julie*. It nearly didn't happen. Professor Evert Sprinchorn, who ran the Drama Department, wasn't at all keen on Atkinson putting on this notoriously difficult play. He thought the students might butcher it. But when he heard Streep read for the part he changed his mind at once.

Miss Julie was very shocking in 1888 when Strindberg wrote it, and managed to remain fairly shocking in 1969. The aristocratic Julie seduces a servant, Jean, purely to prove she can do so. They make love, and her ultimate shame leads to her committing suicide, slashing her wrists with her father's razor. Atkinson noted that Streep, 'played Miss Julie with a voluptuousness that was almost shocking in someone her age.' Sprinchorn was converted. 'After about 10 minutes, I saw that Meryl was just outstanding. It hit you right in the eye.' He looked across the small auditorium at Atkinson and silently nodded. Jean Arthur, Frank Capra's favourite actress in films such as *Mr Smith Goes to Washington*, came to Vassar as a visiting professor when she was nearly 70. She, too, spotted Streep. 'It was like watching a movie star,' she said.

It was Streep's good fortune that her drama teacher had been invited to direct a production at the Cubiculo Theatre in New York during the Spring break. The Cubiculo – Spanish for 'cubicle' – was a small theatre where experimental dance and drama could be performed in the centre of New York. Atkinson agreed to direct Tirso de Molina's *The Playboy of Seville*, the first play to immortalise the legend of Don Juan and the basis of Mozart's opera *Don Giovanni*. Streep now had the chance to perform off-Broadway. She was 22.

The next year Streep was awarded a hard fought for place on the Honours Exchange Program with Dartford College in Hanover, New Hampshire. She added play-writing and set and costume design to her acting studies.

In 1971 she graduated 'cum laude' from Vassar. Twelve short years later, she was invited back to give the Honoured Commencement Address to the graduating students, their families, friends and faculty. It was not so distant in her past that it was just a golden memory. This is part of what she said:

'I came to Vassar from a co-ed public high school in suburban New Jersey. I was a nice girl, pretty,

7

athletic, and I'd read maybe seven books in four years of high school. I read the *New Yorker* and *Seventeen* magazine, had a great vocabulary, and no understanding whatsoever of mathematics and science. I had a way of imitating people's speech that got me A.P. (Advanced Placement) in French without really knowing any grammar. I was not what you would call a natural scholar. Mostly, I was interested in boys, and I enrolled at Vassar when everyone here was female. I think that fact was the single most important catalyst for change in my life to that point. Change in thinking, change and growth of mind and imagination.

Vassar was full of nerds, the idiosyncratic strange ones, the smart weird ones, the undatables. It had its share of high school big shots, too, like me, but we all sank or swam together. The spawning grounds were in New Haven and elsewhere, the sexual competition was far removed. I felt absolutely great in this atmosphere, and I blossomed. I made female friends, ones whom I actually trusted.

The men came in my junior and senior years. I think we were ready for them, but I know I was personally grateful for the two-year hiatus from the sexual rat race.

During my senior year, I went to Dartmouth for a term and experimented with being the outsider in coeducation. There were 60 of us and 6,000 men; that's a true statistic. The shock of that experience was an unexpected one. I got straight A's. My eyes crossed when I got the print-out. At Vassar they had a party in the English department when the first A was given out in 20 years.

I came back to graduate from Vassar with great faith in the integrity of the degree and a strong sense of myself. I had confidence in what the college had given me: the tools for decision-making, and the arrogance to think they might be the right decisions for me in Real Life.

I postponed Real Life, however, for three years. I went, instead, to Yale, to graduate school, and I saw co-education change what I'd known of undergraduate life at that institution for the better. It seemed to me both Vassar and Yale had swallowed the change and come out without changing what was best and most nurturing of individual minds and talents.

I've told you this tale of my time at Vassar because what everybody says is absolutely true. These are, or these were, the halcyon days. Real Life is actually a lot more like high school. The common denominator prevails. Excellence is not always recognized or rewarded. What we watch on our screens, whom we elect, is determined to a large extent by public polls. Looks count. A lot. And unlike the best of the college experience, when ideas and solutions somehow seem attainable if you just get up early, stay up late, try hard enough, and find the right source or method, things on the outside sometimes seem vast and impossible, and settling, resigning oneself, or hiding and hunkering down becomes the best way of getting along.'

There was something wistful in her words. She had been in the limelight for just over five years, a star after her Oscars for *Kramer vs. Kramer* and *Sophie's Choice*, but the sub-text of her speech indicated she had stepped out of a comfort zone at college to which she knew – and regretted – she could never return. This was underlined by the intensity of the speech, very unlike the one I witnessed Muhammad Ali giving at Harvard Commencement where he began: 'I'm very flattered in coming here because I left high school with a D Minus average and they only gave me the Minus because I'd won a gold medal in the Olympics.'

After her graduation, Streep successfully auditioned for the Green Mountain Guild, a Repertory Company in Woodstock, Vermont. It was, at $48 a week, not a highly-paid job, and she supplemented her income by working as a waitress at the Hotel Somerset in Somerville. They performed short pieces by Shaw and Chekhov in school auditoriums and ski lodges. 'We lived in this beautiful house donated to us by an old lady who supported artists. We did little three character plays. You could hear the snoring at the bar and the snowmobiles outside. I directed some. I sold ads for some. I knew that something was being born.'

Streep stayed on with the Green Mountain Guild as the December snows fell, but her intuition told her that, despite having been drowned in plaudits, and even having acted in New York, she was not ready to be born into her Real Life. 'I knew that it was not going to be enough to be an actress in the snows of Vermont. If I was going to do this thing, I ought to do it right. I decided to go to grad school.'

Perhaps she also looked at the productions occupying Broadway theatres in the early 70s: *No, No, Nanette!*, *Hello, Dolly!*, *Pippin*, *Grease*, *Man of la Mancha*, *Fiddler on the Roof* ... and so on. Not a lot of work there for a serious actress. Streep's thoughts turned back to Yale University.

Here came the major turning point in the young Streep's life. Just five years earlier Robert Brustein, a highly academic critic and playwright, had completely revolutionised Yale Drama School. In the face of fierce opposition from the university, he turned it from a largely theoretical academic institution into an almost professional Repertory Theatre. He produced many new plays and, more importantly, revolutionary new inter-pretations of the classics. Streep prudently reprised her *Streetcar* breakdown for him and obtained a scholar-ship for three years. To achieve greatness you usually require great teachers or role models and Streep found hers in Brustein.

A pair of her fellow students, Christopher Durang and Albert Innaurato, had written a cheeky comedy, *The Brothers Karamazov starring Dame Edith Evans*. Innaurato would come in front of the curtain before each performance and announce that, unfortunately, Dame Edith had fallen and broken her hip and would be unable to appear that night. (In fact she was 3,000 miles away, 91 years old and had never heard of the project.) So Innaurato himself would take over the role of the 80-year-old Dame who was to have played the role of Constance Garnett, famed translator of Doestoevsky's play. When it went into Rep, Streep took over the part, and played it in a wheelchair, in what was, in essence, a cabaret. Durang played Aloysha, a monk. Her portrayal of Garnett caught the attention of *The New York Times* critic, Mel Gussow, who noted that her depiction of this 'babbling, decrepit old crone was a daring performance.'

Brustein wrote in his memoirs: 'Meryl whirled about the stage in an antique wheelchair pushed by her mute lover, Ernest Hemingway, badgering the other characters, chattering incessantly about the genteel marvels of literature, and finally transforming into Miss Haversham from *Great Expectations* in order to assail Alyosha (transformed into Pip) about his crude manners and lack of education. Meryl was totally disguised in this part. Her aquiline nose was turned into a witch's beak with a wart on the end, her lazy eyes were glazed with ooze, her lovely voice crackled with savage authority. This performance immediately suggested she was a major actress. Her behaviour in the curtain call alone was worth the price of admission as she rolled her wheelchair through the audience, shouting at the spectators "Go home ... go home!"'

Streep made intensive use of her three years at Yale, participating in more than 30 productions. The experience was greater than any one teacher could give. 'There's no substitute for Rep, where I could play the lead one night, and a robot the next, where you had to turn on a dime. It's a shame that there's much too little of it in this country, because that's where an actor can really find herself. It's what I came up in and all that I know.'

In another Tennessee Willams' play, *Summer and Smoke*, a contemporary of Streep, Robert Lewis, recalled that her Alma 'was certainly the best I ever saw that part played, and that's a reaction you don't usually feel when students do scenes. It was like looking into somebody else's life.'

She certainly made an impression on her fellow students. Joe Grifasi remembers one Rep production where an actor missed his cue, leaving Streep alone on the stage with no lines. 'The setting was a psychiatrist's office and Meryl walked around, picking up objects and finally peering intently at the Rorschach inkblot pictures on the wall. Then she looked at the audience as if she had discovered a major flaw in her character, and burst into tears.' She also had a considerable sense of fun, doing a hilarious John Wayne impression in Christopher Durang's *A Royal Pardon*, and appearing in the chorus of his and Wendy Wasserstein's musical *When Dinah Shore Ruled the Earth*.* Christopher and Wendy were both among the twelve students selected

---

*Dinah Shore was a star singer of the Big Band Era, famous for her television talk shows in the 70s and her relationship with Burt Reynolds, 20 years her junior.

to spend the summer writing at the Eugene O'Neill National Playwriting School, and Streep came along to help with the readings at the end of the course.

Streep left Yale in 1975 with a Master's in Fine Arts and, after seven years' acting training, a perfect pedigree. Brustein could see how special she was. He would even involve her in the appointments of new teachers and wrote, wistfully: 'Meryl appeared in six out of the seven Rep productions in her third year. Perhaps we were unfair to her to feature her so prominently at the expense of her fellow students. She suffered, as a result, from considerable exhaustion as well as considerable envy and jealousy, which brought her close to an ulcer.'

Streep remembers this with pain. When an interviewer – not me – asked her what caused the ulcer, she screamed back: 'The tension! You have to compete against other people for every part. I had 12 to 15 characters that I had to crawl inside of every year. I would tell the teachers "I can't do it any more, I'm going to throw up from the pressure" and they would say, "Pressure? Pressure? You wait till you get out of here, then you'll have problems."'

She also visited a psychiatrist. There was a logical reason for her nervousness. 'Every year there would be a coup d'état,' she recalled. 'The new guy would come in and say: "Whatever you learned last year, don't worry about it. This is going to be a completely new approach." That kind of grab-bag, eclectic education is invaluable... Half the time you're thinking, I wouldn't do it that way, this guy is full of crap. But, in a way, that's how you build up what you believe in. Still, those years made me tired, crazy, nervous. I was constantly throwing up from the pressure.'

But Brustein is certain. 'I am convinced that Meryl's experience in her third year at Yale was a key element in her future success.' He begged her to stay on but she sensed that, out in the real world, she had an appointment with destiny.

She was fearful of the mass audition conducted by the Theatre Communications Group which every drama graduate attended. She ducked it and went to see Rosemarie Tichler, Joe Papp's assistant at New York's Public Theater. 'Why didn't you go to the TCG auditions?' Tichler asked her. 'Stomach trouble,' Streep replied.

The Public Theater was almost the only place in New York City that was consistently producing quality theatre and did not rely on long-running musicals. But the paradox was that by the middle of 1975 its charmed existence was entirely due to the longest-running American musical ever – *A Chorus Line*. This musical about auditions had been work-shopped at the Nickolaus Exercise Center in January 1974. A gifted director, Michael Bennett, saw its potential and brought it to Joe Papp. The Public Theater did not have nearly enough money to put on the show. So they had to borrow $1.6 million. It opened there in May 1975 where immediately, through word of mouth, it sold out. When it transferred to the Schubert Theatre on 25th July 1975, it was already the Broadway equivalent of a gold mine.

Since 1954 Papp had been bringing Shakespeare to

the people with his New York Shakespeare Festival in Central Park, later making use of the outdoor Delacorte Theater, which the city owned. But Papp wanted a permanent home and, by brilliantly pulling together finance from sponsors, in 1967 established The Public Theater on the site of the old Astor Library on Lafayette Street in the East Village. Its location enabled him to charge lower prices, so making the theatre accessible.

Papp told me Streep's reputation had already reached his ears so when she came knocking at his door in 1975, he let her join his stable of other discoveries: Mandy Patinkin, Kevin Kline, the late Raul Julia and David Mamet. Her timing was perfect as he was about to revive a production of Sir Arthur Wing Pinero's drama about actors, *Trelawny of the Wells*. Papp cast her as the stage manager, Imogen, opposite John Lithgow, Mandy Patinkin and Mary Beth Hurt, who played Rose Trelawney, the star of Sadler's Wells.

It was Hurt who was nominated for a Tony. It was Streep whose phone began to ring.

One call was from T. Edward Hambleton who ran The Phoenix Theatre, inviting her to play in a double bill: *Memory of Two Mondays* and *27 Wagons Full of Cotton*. Hambleton, like Streep a graduate of Yale, was the son of a banking family. His passion was producing but, after a few Broadway flops, he set up The Phoenix in the old Yiddish Art Theater on Second Avenue and 12th Street. It left its Lower East Side home in 1961 and moved to a 300-seat theatre on East 74th Street where Hambleton and his partner, Norris Houghton (who later became Head of Drama at Vassar), offered work to other 'Yalies', including Christopher Durang and Wendy Wasserstein.

Arthur Miller's *Memory of Two Mondays* focused on automobile workers trying to make a living during the Depression. Streep played a secretary. She was able to display her talents with greater élan in the other half of the evening in Tennessee Williams' *27 Wagons Full of Cotton*. Streep played a fat, Southern 'retard' and was rewarded with amazed reviews, the Outer Critics Circle Prize, a Theatre World Award and, even, a Tony nomination.

The acting world was now her oyster. She was flown to London to meet Fred Zimmerman to be considered for the role of Julia in *Julia* (1976). This was based on Lillian Hellman's pretentiously named memoir, 'Pentimento'; it was a story she heard from someone else and hijacked for herself, so the idea of an artist painting over an object in his canvas (the meaning of pentimento) may have been a hint. Jane Fonda (who had fleetingly attended Vassar eleven years before Streep) played the eponymous heroine, and Zimmerman's wish prevailed over the American studio wisdom to cast his beloved Vanessa Redgrave as Hellman.

Zimmerman was the most courtly of directors and used his charm when dealing with the Hollywood studios, rather than any table-thumping. Once, when a young Fox executive asked him for his credits, Fred, who had directed *High Noon* and *A Man for All Seasons*, quietly responded: 'You first.'

Both Redgrave and Fonda were more than ten years older than Streep, so she was relegated to the role of Lillian Hellman's bitchy friend. Fonda took pity on her and asked Douggie Slocombe, the English cameraman, to give her as much light as the leads. But Streep's well-lit performance mainly ended up on the cutting-room floor. Jane Fonda vouchsafed to her director: 'This one will go far.'

At the same time Streep started to work in television. She was the wife of ice-hockey player, Michael Moriarty, in *That Championship Season*. Moriarty's character is accused of manslaughter when a member of an opposing team is killed – something which has often appeared to me to be one of the aims of the game.

The soft tongue of Joe Papp then lured Streep to the Delacorte Theatre to play Katherine – 'Your majesty shall mock at me. I cannot speak your England' – in *Henry V*. Michael Moriarty was The Chorus and Paul Rudd the king.

Off-stage romance blossomed for Streep in the alternating production, *Measure for Measure*, where Angelo, a one-man Viennese vice squad, lusts after the virgin, Isabella. John Holland Cazale played Angelo.

Cazale was born in Boston in 1935 and studied at Boston University. All four of his grandparents were Sicilian so he was a true Italian-American. As a teenager he forged a lifelong friendship with another such – Al Pacino.

Cazale studied drama at university and, after a spell in regional theatre, decided to try his luck in New York and went to work there – initially as a messenger, then a taxi driver.

He persisted and he had talent. In January 1968 he was cast, with Pacino, in *The Indian Wants the Bronx*, a one-act play by Israel Horovitz, which ran off-Broadway for six months. Cazale, always the character actor, was the Indian who is set upon by two hooligans for his lack of English and failure to conform to the hooligans' idea of what an American should be.

Pacino won an Obie as Best Actor for his role as the lead thug, and Cazale one for Best Supporting Actor. The good friends continued to play off each other on the stage in *The Local Stigmatic* and Brecht's *Arturo Ui*.

When Pacino got his major break, in the Oscar-laden *The Godfather* (1972), he persuaded the director, Francis Ford Coppola, to audition Cazale who was subsequently cast as Pacino's younger brother. Coppola was so enamoured of Cazale that he made him Gene Hackman's henchman in *The Conversation* (1974). But before that, as if to prove there was no nepotism involved, Cazale got a Best Supporting Actor nomination for *The Godfather Part II* (1974).

So it took all of Joe Papp's powers to persuade this Hollywood player to take on an underpaid part in the park. Cazale was to play the unscrupulous Angelo in *Measure for Measure*. He is given the task of cleaning up Vienna and sentences Claudio to death for making a woman pregnant. But Angelo is not that virtuous himself and wants to sleep with Claudio's stunning sister, Isabella, who has ambitions to become a nun. Angela says he will pardon her brother if she makes love to him. She refuses.

In real life, Streep slept with Cazale after the cast party on the first night of the play. He was 41 and she was 27 but, during rehearsals, they had fallen in love. They moved in together in his Upper West Side apartment. And Mary Louise Streep changed her name – not to Cazale, but to 'shining sea' – Meryl, from the French *mer* for sea.

In the closing lines of *Measure for Measure*, The Duke says:

So bring us to our palace; where we'll show
What's yet behind, that's meet you all should know.

What was next for Streep was the opening of an enchanted door into the world of movies.

2

Caring for Cazale

I once sat at the same table as the Bee Gees' manager, Robert Stigwood, at a Variety Club awards ceremony. The band was being sued by a fellow in Chicago who claimed the melody of their 1977 song 'How Deep is Your Love?' had been stolen from his unreleased 1975 song 'Let It End'. I asked Stigwood why the man was bothering to sue. The mogul shrugged his shoulders with the aphorism: 'Where there's a hit, there's a writ.'

In cinema where there's a hit there is frequently a long list of people who say it was their idea. Take *The Deer Hunter* (1978) in which Streep played Linda, the Pennsylvania steel-town girl who ultimately becomes involved with Michael, played by Robert De Niro. It was her first major film part, so who was responsible for this multi-Oscar-winning film?

It was originally Quinn Redeker's idea. He was a writer who read an article in *Life Magazine* in 1971 about a man making his living from betting on Russian Roulette. Three years later he put the idea to another writer, Lou Garfunkle, who saw the story as a metaphor for Vietnam. So together they wrote *The Men Who Came to Play*, about an air force major who makes money out of an injured 'grunt' by betting on him playing Russian Roulette, with a doctored revolver.

They got it to an agent, Robert Littman, who found the big studios were not keen on such a sensitive theme. So Redeker sold it very cheaply ($19,000) to a couple of Brits – Barry Spikings and Michael Deeley – who had just taken over EMI. After a while they contacted the William Morris Agency to try and find a director. The agency suggested Michael Cimino who had just written and directed *Thunderbolt and Lightfoot*, one of Clint Eastwood's least successful films.

According to Deeley, Cimino had a meeting with Redeker and Garfunkle which was a bit of a disaster as Cimino told them there was no need for any Russian Roulette in the film – which was, of course, the whole point. He sat down with Deeley and Spikings for two hours and told them his concept for an entirely different Vietnam film ... at the end of which, according to Cimino, they chorused: 'Go make it!' – not a phrase that many Englishmen might use.

The result was a hybrid, with Cimino's tale of Pennyslvania steel-mill camaraderie buckled on to Redeker and Garfunkle's Russian Roulette. It could have been a mess but the person who *really* made *The Deer Hunter* was Robert De Niro.

I know this because Streep told me so. De Niro cast her and all the leading men in the movie. Cimino, with fellow-writer Deric Washburn, had turned the story from an officer manipulating a fellow POW to that of

22

three young men who go to war. Powerful as the Russian Roulette may have been, it was the bonding between the working-class heroes that made this film exceptional.

Spikings and Deeley needed a top talent as their leading man and De Niro, with *The Godfather: Part II* (1974) and *Taxi Driver* (1976) under his belt was as top as they came. He had a tough agent (is there an agent who isn't tough in Hollywood?), Harry Ufland, who told them they would have to fork out $1.5 million if they wanted his client, although De Niro's true asking price was less than $1 million. But they got their money's worth as De Niro pretty well took over production of the film.

He went to visit Pennsylvania steel-towns with Cimino and, while the latter looked for locations that would make for unpretty pictures, De Niro studied the lives of the men who lived there. He was so impressed by one of them, Chuck Aspergen, clad in asbestos clothing as he slaved before a fiery furnace, that he cast him as a steelworker in the movie.

De Niro had long known John Cazale, who was a star of Central Park in Joe Papp's Shakespeare productions. Cazale was an excellent ensemble player, often taking on the part of the weakest member of the team. De Niro asked him to come on board as Stan.

Cazale mentioned to him that his girl friend, Meryl Streep, would come home and have him in stitches with her impersonation of Andrea Serban, the Romanian director of *The Cherry Orchard* which was playing at the Lincoln Center. De Niro went to see Chekhov's tragi-comedy for himself. He knew Streep by reputation but was utterly swept away by her performance as Dunyasha, the maid. It was a comic triumph; she did a prat-fall every time she came on stage – 'to amuse myself – and the rest of the cast'. This girl could do anything, so he invited her to play Linda, eventually his love-interest in *The Deer Hunter*. She was delighted to be in a film with De Niro but, more especially, with John. Tragically it was to be their first and last movie together.

Rather like Yul Brynner rounding up the other six in *The Magnificent Seven*, De Niro chose the magnificent others for *The Deer Hunter*. What was unique in his method was that he cast mainly from the Broadway stage. He would have known of Christopher Walken as Annie Hall's nutty brother, Dwayne, who tells Alvy of his unfortunate desire to drive into the headlights of oncoming cars at night. (It's a very clever set-up to put Woody into just such jeopardy later in the movie.) Christopher Walken used to be Ronald Walken and was primarily a dancer, although he once took a summer out to be a lion-tamer's assistant. He was born in the same year as De Niro, who went to see him act opposite Geraldine Paige in Tennessee Williams' *Sweet Bird of Youth* at the Harkness Theatre. Walken played the part of Chance Wayne, first played by Paul Newman. Wayne has returned to the Gulf Coast town where he once gave venereal disease to the daughter of a town boss, and now faces impending castration.

De Niro had found his Nick, the emotionless 'grunt'

who plays professional Russian Roulette, and Walken found security. He had never earned more than $11,000 for a job before, and *The Deer Hunter* paid $14,000. But he was rewarded with more than that. Back in his hotel bed after attending the Academy Awards he clasped his Oscar for Best Supporting Actor to his chest and said to his wife: 'This will buy our house.'

The posse was completed with John Savage. He was playing the part of the victim in David Mamet's *American Buffalo* at the St Clement's Theater, New York. He was to be a victim again in *The Deer Hunter*, going through all manner of ordeals, including possibly the most terrifying pause in cinema history while he waits to pull the trigger in a game of Russian Roulette, which he has been forced to play. His character, Steven, eventually ends up in a veterans' hospital with his legs amputated.

The fundamental art of the film lay in the casting. De Niro didn't consider friends like Al Pacino or Michael Moriarty because they would have upset the careful balance of the group. And he knew that Streep could be one of the boys.

But Streep's role is more than that – or became more than that. She told me that much of her part as Linda consisted of blank spaces in the script. Cimino told her: 'Just say what you think she would say.'

Streep laughed: 'I kinda liked that. But it did make me nervous.'

What came across was an artless and not very articulate girl who worked in the grocery store of a bleak Pennsylvania steel town, where the men toiled at the mills, and beer and week-end deer-hunting and girl-chasing provided their only release. 'I knew a lot of girls like that in New Jersey. They're 'waiters' – they wait to be asked for a date, wait to be asked to marry, wait for their boyfriends to come home from war,' Streep recalled.

At the party in the American Legion Hall to celebrate the wedding of Steven to the pregnant Angela and the departure of the boys for Vietnam, Linda is the girl friend of Nick (Christopher Walken), but subtly indicates her attraction to Michael (De Niro). Her pratfalls as Dunyasha stood her in good stead at the drunken dance. She moves into Nick's mobile home when he, Michael and Steven go off to war. While they experience a hell-on-earth in Vietnam, she symbolises the infinitely-preferable drudgery of life at home.

I saw *The Deer Hunter* in a stunned preview theatre in Soho. There were drinks afterwards and the guitarist, John Williams, asked me if I thought he should have let them use his 'Cavatina' in what had seemed to him to be a pro Americans-in-Vietnam film. But it hadn't seemed like that to me: it was about courage, comrade-ship and the utter madness of war, so brilliantly symbolised by the use of Russian Roulette.

When, at the end, they bury Nick in his home town, and Linda begins to sing 'God Bless America' and all, even the limbless Steven, join in this intensely patriotic song, it is so moving because this is precisely what such men and women would do. They are no questioning liberals; they are unquestioning patriots.

The film won five Oscars, including Best Director and Best Picture, and was nominated for four more, including De Niro as Best Actor in a Leading Role and Streep as Best Actress in a Supporting Role.

Few people realised just how great her support for John Cazale had been during the months of filming. While she was still in *The Cherry Orchard*, John had fallen ill with what turned out to be bone cancer which was, inevitably, fatal. She had already begun to look after him at their apartment. When De Niro had invited Cazale to play Stan, the hunter who stayed at home, John accepted. But then he had to break the news of his cancer to Cimino before they started to film. He said he would have to have radiation treatment and quite understood if they wanted to cast somebody else.

Cimino, true to the ethic of the film, stood by him. EMI did not. They couldn't get medical insurance for John so they asked Cimino to write an alternative script in case he died during filming. Harsh words were exchanged before the director finally declined. Streep made it clear that if John was not in the film, neither was she. EMI wisely backed down. Cazale lived to see the end of shooting, with Streep nursing him. But she had signed up to go to Austria after the film to play in the NBC mini-series *Holocaust*.

John Cazale urged Streep to go. She still had a substantial student loan from Yale to pay off. 'I did it for the money. I needed it very badly, and I make no bones about that,' she said at the time.

In *Holocaust* Streep plays Inga Helms Weiss, the German-Catholic wife who voluntarily follows her Jewish husband, Karl (James Woods), into a concentration camp. The filming ran weeks over schedule, lasting more than two and a half months, and the atmosphere on the set was doubly depressing as someone had decided they should film on the site of the Mauthausen Concentration Camp in Upper Austria. At one point the veteran English actor Cyril Shaps announced: 'I don't think I can go on.' But he did. And so did Streep.

The same director, Marvin J. Chomsky, had directed the mini-series *Roots* – based on Alex Haley's questionable genealogical memoir for ABC, creating a record audience of over 160 million viewers. NBC hoped *Holocaust* would deliver the same, which it nearly did, with 120 million. It also had an enormous impact in Germany when it was aired there in 1979, introducing the country to the word 'holocaust', which had been hitherto unknown. After the 'Krystallnacht' episode which covered the night of 9th November 1938 when the Reich ordered loyal Germans to ransack Jewish businesses and destroy their synagogues, dozens of Germans telephoned their local Police Stations to confess that they had taken part in the atrocity.

Much of what money Streep might have made on the mini-series was used up in calls to Cazale in New York. And by her lover's hospital bills. He had been moved into Sloan-Kettering Cancer Center. When Streep saw him on her return from Austria he had lost thirty pounds. She immediately put her work on hold and moved in with him there.

Joe Papp had, in a way, been the midwife of their coming together and observed the couple in the final months. He told me: 'She took care of him as if there were nobody else on earth. She was always at his side. It was such a statement of loyalty and commitment She never betrayed any notion that he would not survive. She gave him tremendous hope. She spent weeks at the hospital while John wasted away. There is no way she can forget a thing like that. It's part of her life now, part of her art.'

John Cazale died on 12th March 1978. He didn't live to see either *The Deer Hunter* or *Godfather III* (1990) where he appeared in flashback. He left a legacy, unique in Hollywood, namely that all the six features which he appeared in – the other two being *The Conversation* (1974) and *Dog Day Afternoon* (1976) – had been nominated for Academy Awards as Best Picture.

Cazale was buried in the Holy Cross Cemetery and Mausoleum in Maiden, Massachusetts. His mother, Cecelia, who died in 1997 at the age of 99, and his sister, Catharine, who died the following year, lie beside him. There is another memorial to him in New York: the McGinn-Cazale Theatre at 2162 Broadway.

Streep said of John: 'I think he was an unsung actor. He made everything mean something. Such good judgment, such uncluttered thought.'

Many years later she admitted: 'John's death is still very much with me. It affects everything that happens

29

afterwards. But, just as a child does, I think you can assimilate the pain and go on without making an obsession of it. We seem to look at sickness, death, grief or adversity as somehow being totally unfair. I don't think people in any other century felt they deserved perfection as much as Americans do in the twentieth century. We seem to think 'Hey, this is not supposed to be happening to me.' I feel lucky when anything goes right.'

Streep threw herself into her work. She said at the time: 'The fame of the show has brought me something surreal. The other day I was riding my bike through Chelsea when these four guys in a Volkswagen started yelling at me out of the window, "Hey, Holocaust, hey, Holocaust!" Can you imagine? It's absurd that that episode in history can be reduced to people screaming out of car windows at an actress.'

Here Miss Streep seemed to be dissembling somewhat. If you are on prime-time television watched by half the nation for four successive nights, you would have to be pretty naïve not to expect some fame, although not necessarily to attract the words shouted from inside – with a certain irony – a Volkswagen. She had already signed up to play Alan Alda's mistress in *The Seduction of Joe Tynan* (1979) and, although she was hardly in the mood for such a part, she was, after all, an actress.

But she did not relish going home to John's apartment where there was no John, so she asked her brother, Harry III, to move in with her. This arrangement was short-lived. After a few weeks a woman turned up at the door, claiming to be a previous girl friend of John's, brandishing a copy of the lease, which was in her name. Streep was shattered. She and her brother had to move out. But fortunately Harry III had a friend from Yale who was travelling in Europe for a month and he agreed to let Streep and her brother stay in his studio in Soho. The friend's name was Don Gummer.

Don Gummer came from Louisville, Kentucky – Muhammad Ali's home town. He had studied art in Indianapolis and married a local girl, Peggy Lucas. Gummer continued his studies in Boston at the School of the Museum of Fine Arts and then went to Yale to do his masters, graduating in 1973.

Gummer's reputation as a sculptor grew during the next five years and in 1978 he had his first solo exhibition. His marriage had come to an end and he was, it is said, involved with a dancer, which possibly accounts for his continuing friendship with her brother, who was a choreographer. Streep had met Don Gummer a couple of times but claimed she hardly knew him. Nevertheless, she wrote him letters while he was off on his travels. Clearly some spark might have been ignited before he left.

But what happened to her when she was living alone in Don's place? Did she get to know him better? Two British psychologists, Sam Gosling and Daniel Miller, once set out to explore one of anthropology's central questions: what is the relationship between people and their possessions? Using students as subjects they observed that if you look at people's homes and possessions in the right way, you can find out what makes them tick. Gosling and Miller asked people to answer certain questions about their friends. Then he asked some strangers to snoop around the bedrooms of the same people. The results were fascinating. If you're somebody's friend, you will have a pretty accurate idea of how extrovert they are, and also how agreeable they are. But with regard to certain other characteristics, the bedroom snoopers came out better than the friends. When it comes to judging how conscientious somebody is, or how emotionally stable, or how open they are to new experiences, it's better to snoop around someone's bedroom for half an hour than to be friends with them for years.

Gummer's place was a shrine to creativity. Streep would have been more than intrigued. She once said she could never be married to a man who was not creative.

On his return, Don told Streep she could stay on and built her a spare room. When she was nominated for an Emmy for *Holocaust*, she announced she would not be attending the ceremony. 'I don't believe performances should be taken out of context for awards,' she announced – not a belief that persisted for very long.

There was probably another reason. Two days before the ceremony, on 15th September 1978, she took Don to her parents' home on Mason's Island, Connecticut and they were married.

One can see the need for keeping it low key: not

only was Don Gummer three and a half years younger than Streep, but it had been only six months since John Cazale died. So they delayed any major celebration with friends until May of the following year.

3

Early Loves

Meryl Streep once said to me: 'The hardest thing to do in film is to make it seem that two people love each other. When one walks into a room, the other goes...' and here she paused to produce a gesture of exhilaration and rapture that is difficult to describe in mere words.

In a curious way, Streep brings such power to the screen that it is only when she has an equally powerful romantic lead opposite her that the chemistry really can begin to work. She isn't Sandra Bullock who can be in love with a man in a coma – *While You Were Sleeping* (1995) – or with a man whom she cannot meet as she is living two years ahead of him – *The Lake House* (2006).

Bullock could make you think she has fallen in love with a tree, but Streep needs to interact, never better than she did with Kevin Kline in *Sophie's Choice* (1982); with Robert Redford in *Out of Africa* (1985); and with Clint Eastwood in *The Bridges of Madison County* (1995), when she was in her mid-forties. All these performances are moving in less than conventional ways.

Streep was nearly 30 when she began to star in films and so the more usual 'young love' movies did not come her way – even if she had wanted them to. Although she bravely soldiered on with *The Seduction of Joe Tynan* after John Cazale's death, the part didn't have enough to nourish her. Alan Alda was famous as Hawkeye in television's 'Mash' and probably wanted to remind the world of his versatility by playing a Senator in the mould of a young Kennedy in a film he wrote himself. Streep is Karen Traynor, a Louisiana lawyer in Washington, who wants to seduce Joe Tynan into supporting her opposition to a Supreme Court nominee. Although it is Joe who suggests sex in a hotel room, there is little doubt as to which of them is pulling the strings. Their lust undoubtedly wins over any deep, emotional involvement and the movie ends up with Joe going back to his wife.

I asked Streep if this was fair. She said it wouldn't have happened if *she* had been writing the script.

She also gave me a shrewd insight into the nature of people's reaction to her in public. 'I was once going through an airport with Alan. Because of the kinds of characters I have usually played in movies, I think people are polite to me but they don't jump on me. But, with Alan, they think he's their brother-in-law. They come up to him and throw their arms around him. 'How ya doing? I saw you last night. You were great.' It's the persona you portray on the screen.'

Sometimes a book just gets under your skin. One Saturday morning I began to read *The Magus* by John

Fowles. I had arranged to eat lunch with friends and planned to do several other things that day ... but remained in bed until I finished the novel. The story of the young Englishman going to a lonely Greek island where he is seduced into a series of 'Godgames' by an alluring blonde fed my young fantasies. When a magazine asked me to do a profile of Fowles, I was on the train to Lyme Regis like a cannonball fired from one of the stately cannons on The Cobb. Streep was soon to make that austere stone harbour-wall world famous in the poster for *The French Lieutenant's Woman* (1981).

For somebody who had written so sensitive and wistful a book, Fowles could be mistaken for the sort of Englishman you would encounter with a pipe and a pint in a refreshment tent at Lords. Indeed, he had been captain of cricket at Bedford School, as well as Head Boy, and had gone on to take a commission in the Royal Marines.

As we walked along The Cobb, Fowles tried to dampen my enthusiasm for *The Magus*, claiming it was a novel of youth, written by a retarded adolescent. The film version, which he scripted, starring Michael Caine and Candice Bergen, turned out to be something of a stinker. Woody Allen memorably remarked: 'If I had to live my life again, I'd do everything the same – except for seeing *The Magus*.'

Fowles searched his dreams for ideas for his novels. In one he had seen a lone young woman in a cloak standing at the end of The Cobb, looking out to sea.

He set himself the task of exploring why she was there and who she was. From these dreams and imaginings emerged *The French Lieutenant's Woman*.

The novel had sold more than 5 million copies and been translated into over 20 languages. Fowles did not want any movie adaptation to go the way of *The Magus*, impairing the reputation of the original work. So he entrusted it to the gifted Czech director, Karel Reisz, who made *Saturday Night and Sunday Morning* (1960) and *Isadora* (1968) with Vanessa Redgrave, whom he wanted to play the French lieutenant's woman. But the money was not forthcoming so the project was postponed. Redgrave's loss proved Streep's good luck. It wasn't any of her films that made Reisz think that she could crack the part, rather her performance as Kate in *The Taming of the Shrew* at Joe Papp's Theater in New York.

Fowles' book is ostensibly a Victorian novel in which the rich Charles, who hopes to marry the equally rich Ernestina, is entranced by a poor young woman, Sarah, whom he sees, staring out to sea. Sarah tells him she is a former governess who was/is in love with the French lieutenant who has betrayed her and gone back to his wife. Maybe he will return, or maybe she is making the whole thing up. Charles takes the hook. But what makes the book very different is that the author is a character within it, commenting on the Victorian age, making reference to its myriad thinkers from Marx to Darwin, and not always able to control his characters. Fowles has a problem, which he explains in chapter 55, while riding with Charles on a train to London. He doesn't know what to do with his story. He can't manipulate the plot 'to show one's readers what one thinks of the world around one' because this story happened 100 years ago and 'we know what has happened since.' The only solution, he decides, is to write two endings.

Very Post-Modernist ... but try and turn it into a film! Several people did try, and none succeeded. Fowles resolutely stayed in the shadows. But the man who cracked it was the playwright and, later, Nobel laureate, Harold Pinter. It was right up his street. He did away with the notion of the author entering the story and came up with the idea of two actors in the present day – Mike and Anna. They are playing Charles and Sarah, and having an affair as well. Pinter's script obscures the borders between the past and the present. At a party at Mike's home, a guest inquires about the film's ending. The actor can't quite remember whether the director has chosen the happy or sad one. At the very end – and this was John Fowles' suggestion – he mistakenly calls 'Anna', 'Sarah'.

Streep, of course, leapt at the part/parts. Every actor loves to play an actor: not only is it a profession they know, but it gives them endless possibilities to improvise. For Streep, it was also a chance to work with great artists, like Reisz and Pinter, who were, like her, vigorously intellectual and creative.

It was a point of pride that she should get the voice of the mysterious Sarah to perfection. 'Karel and Harold said she should have the accent of a woman who was trying to better herself,' she told me. 'Something you couldn't locate in a specific vicinity, something that was proper and correct but had no region. When I've come to London and seen people doing American accents' – she dropped into a broad Brooklyn voice – 'everybody's talking like this. But people don't. There are all sorts of different accents. So I worked with Barbara Markham who was a brilliant dialogue coach. I didn't want to offend anybody here.'

Streep made a point of not actually going through any of her lines from the film with the late Mrs Markham but instead would read from period books such as *Persuasion* by Jane Austen, an appropriate choice since it includes scenes on The Cobb at Lyme.

With a Pinter script and Streep's star in the ascendant, Reisz got backing from United Artists to fund the film. He chose to economise in the case of Charles by not casting an established film star, but a promising one. Jeremy Irons was well known for his stage work: from playing John the Baptist in *Godspell* to Leontes in *The Winter's Tale* at Stratford. Such a contrast between good and evil would stretch most actors but Irons showed himself the master of both roles and had landed a much sought-after part, another Charles – Charles Ryder – in the television series *Brideshead Revisited*. When Reisz asked him to play opposite Streep after he finished that, it seemed a dream come true for the 31-year-old actor.

But it turned into a nightmare.

I spent a bit of time with Jeremy Irons in the spring of 1984 when he was on Broadway with Glenn Close in Tom Stoppard's *The Real Thing*. An agent had got a commission from a publisher for a book on Irons.(It didn't happen; the agent ran away with the money.) But we did have some interesting preliminary chats and one night, after his performance, Irons was granted the Robert Benchley table at the 21 Club and told me how his chance to act with Streep very nearly didn't happen.

Brideshead had been hit by a television technicians' strike, and shooting stopped for nearly three months. When they started work again it was evident that they would go badly over schedule. Jeremy warned the producer he had signed to do a movie with Reisz in March. The producer told him that that was fine and they would work it out. But later the television company, Granada, informed him that they would not release him for the film. Relying on his verbal agreement with the producer, Jeremy went to see a lawyer in London who said he would win, but it would take more than a year for such a case to come to court. And by that time, of course, *The French Lieutenant's Woman* would be completed.

Irons was distraught. By that stage about eight million pounds had been spent on *Brideshead*. But after a few drinks he wrote to Sir Denis Forman, the chairman of Granada, saying that he would quit the series unless, by 6 pm the following day, they agreed to release him to make the film. He wrote: 'I know you can bar me

41

from the union, I know you can sue me. My house is worth £85,000. That's about all I have. I'm not a hysterical actor – I'm just an actor against the wall.'

The deadline came and went, but there was no reply from Sir Denis. And so Irons didn't turn up for work the following day. He had walked off the set of one of the most expensive productions in British television. But two days later the Granada chairman invited him to tea. Sir Denis said he felt very let down. Jeremy said *he* felt very let down, so they were both in the same boat. Sir Denis could see the young actor meant business and asked if he would return to work if Granada could sort things out in three weeks. Jeremy breathed a sigh of relief. In the event the film paid for the down time in the television schedule – and Granada invested in the film.

Streep knew nothing of this when she arrived in Lyme Regis along with her husband, Don, and their four month old baby, Henry – also known as Gippy. They stayed with the rest of the cast and crew in a local inn where she breastfed her child during the early weeks of shooting.

John Fowles had given her just one note about Sarah – via Harold Pinter – and that was 'keep her inexplicable.' And this she duly did, further adding to her character's mystique with not a single interview while she was concentrating on her work.

Jeremy Irons was understandably nervous about acting opposite her – twice in one film – not least because this was his first major movie. Irons recalled a scene in the barn when Sarah wakes up and he has been watching over her. 'It wasn't going well after many takes. So Meryl came over to me and physically shook me and said: 'It's hard, it's hard. You have to do it, though, it's never easy.' She was never satisfied. She was a tigress biting at my ankles, gnawing at a problem until she found a solution. She is strong and opinionated and nearly always right.'

Pauline Kael of *The New Yorker*, to some the doyenne of film critics, and certainly one of the most controversial, just didn't care for Streep. 'We never really get into the movie because, as Sarah, Meryl Streep gives an immaculate, technically accomplished performance, but she isn't mysterious. She's pallid and rather glacial,' Kael wrote, 'there's no passion ... her technique doesn't add up to anything.'

Those words hurt and haunted Streep down the years. Maybe part of her sensed that the critic had a point. Her anger, however, erupted with surprising bile. 'I'm incapable of not thinking about what Pauline wrote,' she later retorted. 'And you know what I think? That Pauline was a poor Jewish girl who was at Berkeley with all these rich Pasadena Wasps with long blonde hair, and the heartlessness of them got her. And then, years later, she sees me.'

With due respect to Kael, Streep is magnificent in the title role. With the art that disguises art, she is able to say one thing while communicating that she may be thinking another. Her revelation to Charles of her rescue of the wounded lieutenant is just such a

43

moment. 'He was in great pain yet he never cried out, not the smallest groan. I admired his courage. I did not know that men can be very brave and then very false' – and then she abstractly picks at her hair as she recalls – 'He told me I was beautiful and he could not understand why I was not married.' True or false? She invites the audience to draw their own conclusion. Even in her private moments when she looks at herself in her mirror and makes angry, self-loathing sketches of herself, we get a hint of the inner turmoil that is usually shrouded by the serene aspect she shows to the world.

Irons makes a distinguished film debut as Charles. Karel Reisz observed when he cast him 'he has something of the Heathcliffe about him.' Jeremy was wise to write that letter to Sir Denis – he knew that if he didn't crack it in movies by his early thirties he never would – for the film ignited a career which took him all the way to the Oscar podium for his portrayal of Claus von Bulow in *Reversal of Fortune* (1990).

Unfortunately the film is hobbled by the clumsy device of Mike and Anna and their affair. One wonders what it brings to the party? Where Fowles had interpolated some challenging philosophy in the 'character' of his present-day self, Mike and Anna seem somewhat vain and vapid creatures. There is something about their lovemaking scene that makes one want to look away. Not an affair to remember.

* * *

You will recall that Robert De Niro launched Streep's Hollywood career when he invited her to appear in *The Deer Hunter*. Well, six years later his career was in trouble and he needed a return favour. It seemed bizarre. Robert De Niro, greatest film star in the world, Oscar winner for his prodigious performance as the tragic boxer, Jake La Motta, in Martin Scorsese's *Raging Bull* (1980) – to some the greatest film of all time – was on the ropes. He had, to be brutal, lost his audience. The American grosses tell the same sad tale: *True Confessions* (1980), where he played a priest, $10m; Sergio Leone's *Once Upon a Time in America* (1984), where he was David 'Noodles' Aaronson, $5m; and Scorsese's *King of Comedy* (1982) in which De Niro gave a flesh-creeping performance as the psycho Rupert Pupkin, a mere $2.5m.

Meanwhile Streep, as they crudely say, had been putting bums on seats. De Niro had lost his family audience and, more importantly, his female audience. Women usually choose which film a couple go to see. After watching him rape both Tuesday Weld and Elizabeth McGovern in the Cannes' screening of *Once Upon a Time in America* a woman informed the star: 'I was deeply embarrassed to be in the cinema. As a woman I was demoralised'. De Niro, reputedly, was so stung by the remark that he retreated to his suite at the Hotel du Cap near Antibes and took no further part in publicity for the film – not that he much likes doing publicity anyway.

Paramount must have been delighted at the prospect of the two *Deer Hunter* stars re-uniting in a new love

45

story entitled, with the obviousness that characterised too many things in the movie, *Falling in Love* (1984). History does not relate how long it took for writer Michael Cristopher to take a long hard look at David Lean's *Brief Encounter* (1945) with its ingredients – Celia Johnson/Trevor Howard/both married/no sex please, we're British/steam trains/Rachmaninoff 2 – and then write his first screenplay. However, it would be charitable to assume it was not very long. Cristopher had won both a Tony and a Pulitzer prize for his moving Broadway play *The Shadow Box* (1977).

Very early in film writing courses, students are taught the need for what is termed a 'meet-cute' in any romance in which the protagonists briefly encounter each other but fail to realise they are destined to fall in love ... *while we, the audience, do.* In Rizzoli's New York book store Molly (Streep) is buying a Christmas present for her husband, a book on sailing, and Frank (De Niro) one on gardening for his wife. They become entangled in the doorway and, de-tangling, each ends up with the other's tome. Nevertheless the merry Christmas period is spent at their respective homes: Molly with her husband, Frank with his wife and children.

Destiny, however, has other plans. They meet again on a commuter train where subtle glances and signals let us know they rather fancy each other. Neither Streep nor De Niro has lost their individual charisma – she looks as lovely as, and not unlike, Princess Di while he has an artisan bashfulness – but the problem is the artless plot that ties them together like gift-wrapping.

When he suggests lunch and she replies: 'No, I'm married,' that is the first and the last lame attempt at a clever exchange. Both have affectionate partners at home but the casting of these supporting parts is somewhat underpowered. Disappointingly the chance for two great actors to play guilt is only glancingly offered.

The Belgian director, Ulu Grosbard (his real name), cleared the set to let the stars do their love scene in a friend's apartment. But Molly, after two buttons of her blouse have been undone, cannot go through with it. Maybe if they had done so, they would have sold more tickets.

De Niro, surprisingly eager to do publicity for this film, explained: 'Love scenes today are done with such facility, such professionalism. People clinch in the same way whether it's out West or in the jungles of Thailand.' Well, yes, there is something universal about the language of love.

More pertinently Streep said: 'We wanted something real, something awkward and crumpled.'

The fact that true love can be more destabilising than a casual fling is the essence of the movie. 'It has something to do with what happens to you in sixth grade,' said Streep in a rather personal aside. 'That's when it happened to me. You turn a corner and you expect to see him, that kind of little, bitty thing. Something that makes you blush. Passion makes you that innocent again.' In the film, both characters have friends who are divorced. Streep shrewdly observed.

47

'We all know marriages where we say: 'What the hell does she see in him?' And with others we say: 'If only I could be like that!' and – boom! They're divorced. There's a corner of their lives that's just waiting. And you don't know it's waiting until it happens.'

The film attracted lukewarm reviews and maybe made enough money to cover the stars' salaries. It was left to his performance as Al Capone in *The Untouchables* a couple of years later for De Niro to regain his natural constituency and a walloping hit.

And yet, when I watched *Falling in Love* for the second time for the purpose of this book, on a DVD, sandwiched between the soaps and *Spooks* on the telly, I found it good entertainment, largely because of the beguiling charisma of the leading couple. Somehow, though, their stardom seemed to overwhelm the opportunity for undiluted screen chemistry. Nowadays, when films are delivered in so many ways – from the premiere to the mobile – some grow and flourish in contexts where there isn't the imperative of a darkened room and gigantic images to demand your attention.

The DVD of *Falling In Love* has apparently provided a bonus income stream for De Niro. In his American Film Institute tribute to Streep at the Lincoln Center, he said he was going to sell DVDs of the movie to people coming out – since so few went in when it was first released.

4

Streep vs. Hoffman

Streep's strengths lay more in playing characters who challenged than in those who conformed. Woody Allen could see that, and cast her in *Manhattan* (1979) as his wife, Jill – a woman who has left her husband to live with another woman, Connie.

When I was at school we had a witty Irish Latin master who loved making us laugh. However, if any pupil dared to attempt a joke in his class, he would reprimand him, 'Leave the funnies to me.' So it is with most Woody Allen comedies; he has all the 'funnies' and the rest of the cast are there to set them up. In *Manhattan*, Woody is a 40-year-old television script-writer who has a 17-year-old girl friend, Tracey (Mariel Hemingway). But he falls for Mary (Diane Keaton), the mistress of his best friend, and they start living together, with disastrous consequences.

Streep told me she knew none of this when she started filming. Woody wouldn't let her – or any other actor – see the script, just the pages they were in – three in her case.

I suggested this seemed somewhat paranoid but she

could see the logic in it, 'He's very protective of his work. Very often films are killed by word of mouth before they even reach the screen ... before anyone has even seen them. "I've heard that that was terrible – don't go!" ' Streep told me.

'It wasn't a really difficult part to play. It wasn't a part I had to invest my heart and soul in to any great measure. Since I didn't see the script I didn't know if I was playing a child molester or what.'

I wondered if she had been able to write some of her own lines as she did in *The Deer Hunter*. Streep laughed. 'No. In fact Woody was on me for where I placed a comma in a sentence. I was nervous about working with him because I admire him so much. I was very deferential at first and I think that's why he got on my case so that I wouldn't be, so that I'd be bitchy towards him. He would concentrate on Diane but in my scenes with him it was an offhand 'just feel it out.' I think he wanted to make me nuts. But it was good fun.'

Manhattan along with *Annie Hall* and *Sleeper* (1973) make up Allen's three most complete comedies. Significantly they were the three films he wrote with Marshall Brickman. There is no real need for an ex-wife in the plot – possibly they wrote it just to get Streep in the film – but it adds some great running gags to the very clever humour.

Nearly all of the Ike/Jill story is told by references to things past when he discovers Jill is writing a book about their marriage. 'You're going to tell everybody

about our sexual life, all the details,' Ike chides her. 'I
was at a party and a guy said he had read a chapter.
I spilt wine on my pants.'

She accuses him of feeling threatened, but he bitterly
denies it.

'Out of the two of us, I was not the psychotic,
immoral, promiscuous one,' he snips sarcastically. 'Did
I leave anything out?'

When Ike goes round to pick up their son, Willy,
for the weekend, Jill tells him that the boy is beginning to show some real talent at drawing. Ike wonders:
'How can that be, as I don't draw and you don't
draw?'

Jill's lover, Connie, comments: 'I draw' and Ike turns
on her with: 'Sure, but there's no way you could be
the actual father.'

When Connie is out of the room, he tells his ex-wife:
'I cannot understand how you can prefer her to me.'

'You knew my history when you married me,' Jill
points out.

'I know,' Ike admits. 'My analyst warned me against
you. But you were so beautiful I got another analyst.'

It transpires that when the two women were consum-
mating their relationship in a cabin, Ike was lurking
outside in his car. He tried to run Connie over when
she emerged. He denies this. 'Have you any idea how
slowly I was going?'

'Not slowly enough to stop you ripping the whole
front porch of the cabin off,' Jill reminds him.

All wonderful noises off. After Ike reads the book

he returns to the apartment with the words: 'I came here to strangle you.'

'Nothing I wrote was untrue,'Jill insists.

He maintains that he comes across 'like Lee Harvey Oswald,' saying she paints him as narcissistic, misanthropic and self-righteous. She tries to mollify him 'I wrote some nice things about you, as well.' But that just turns out to be that Ike cries when he watches *Gone with the Wind*.

There's also a politically incorrect allusion to the possible sexual orientation of little Willy, Ike and Jill's son. In their first scene together Ike asks Jill: 'How's Willy? Does he play baseball? Does he wear dresses?' Later on, as he is about to leave the apartment, her lesbian lover reminds Jill: 'Don't forget that Willy's at ballet class.'

Streep, with angry long hair which she strokes like a contemptuous lioness and the height to look haughtily down on her ex, plays off Woody just wonderfully. The comic timing that looked like artifice in the slapstick entangled in store-door sequence with De Niro in *Falling in Love* flows joyously in the hands of an actor/director in his prime. What a shame they didn't work together again.

Streep is reported to have said: 'On a certain level the film offends me because it's about all these people's neuroses.' And, if she said that and if that's what it was about, that's about as good a definition of a Woody Allen movie as you can get.

* * *

Instead of Woody, another small Jewish man was to become her most successful foil to date. In certain respects the careers of Dustin Hoffman and Meryl Streep were somewhat similar; in others, very different. Both made their name on the New York stage before they made it in cinema – Hoffman won an Obie in 1966 for playing a 43-year-old, spinsterish Russian clerk in Ronald Ribman's *The Journey of the Fifth Horse*. Both were 30, relatively old, before they made their mark in movies, and both owed a lot to Mike Nichols, who cast Dustin in *The Graduate* (1967) – a big break that nearly didn't happen.

Hoffman told me that he was playing in Henry Livings' *Eh?* in New York when the call came from Nichols in Los Angeles. 'I said to him that I did not think I was right for the role and he said: 'Why?' and I said: 'Well, he's a kind of Anglo-Saxon, tall, slender, good-looking chap.' He said: 'And you're Jewish.' And I said: 'That's right. Short and Jewish.' He said: 'Well, inside, Benjamin Braddock is short and Jewish.'

Hoffman came from the other side of the tracks from Streep – his father was a prop man in the movies – his education was not comparable to Vassar and Yale. Hoffman dropped out of a medical course at Santa Monica City College and took acting classes at the Pasadena Playhouse. When he came to New York it was to work as a medical orderly; he spent two years and made five attempts to get into Lee Strasberg's Actors' Studio.

Yet on a cool March day in 1974, it was Streep who

53

came to audition before Hoffman, along with his director, Robert Benton, and producer, Stanley Jaffe. Hoffman had a contract giving him complete artistic control over *Kramer vs Kramer*. He had wanted the actress he was then dating, Kate Jackson – the brunette from *Charlie's Angels* – to play the part of his wife. But ABC television would not release her from her contract and she was not inclined to do a 'Jeremy Irons' and break it.

Sherry Lansing, then working at Columbia Pictures (backers of the film) and who was later to become the first female President of Twentieth Century Fox, suggested they see Streep. Neither *The Deer Hunter* nor *The Seduction of Joe Tynan* nor *Manhattan* had come out, so they were considering her, not for Mrs Kramer, but for Phyllis, a lawyer who has a one night stand with the abandoned Kramer.

'I thought I was going for the wife's part,' Streep recalled, 'so I launched right in to how I thought about her and the film and they were looking at each other sideways. Nobody told me that I was there for the smaller part of Phyllis. I only learned that later.'

In fact it's doubtful if she would have played Phyllis, whose big moment is to encounter Kramer's little son when she is walking down the corridor naked. Streep doesn't do naked. JoBeth Williams did the part, which had been more substantial when Streep read the script.

Nevertheless, Streep was called back for another meeting with two of the wise men, this time with the role of Joanna Kramer firmly in their minds. Benton recalls: 'It was one of those classic scenes where everything went wrong. Dustin and I walked in late and the three of us didn't hit it off at all. As soon as he and I got back on the street, though, we realised she was the girl for us.'

Why was a fellow actor deciding whether or not Streep should have a part in the film? Hoffman had made up for a late start in the movies by a meteoric ascent: Ratso Rizzo in *Midnight Cowboy* (1969), Carl Bernstein in *All the President's Men* (1976) and 'Babe' Levy in *Marathon Man* (1976) (with Laurence Oliver providing free dental treatment) had paved his way to power. Control was something Hoffman craved. In 1971, he had joined First Artists Productions – a company set up by Paul Newman, Sidney Poitier, Barbra Streisand and, later, Steve McQueen – with a deal that gave him a million dollars a movie, 50% of its box-office revenue, creative control and final say on editing. This 'my bat, my ball' contract was pretty onerous for anybody working with him. And so it proved in *Kramer vs. Kramer*.

When I first met Dustin Hoffman in a very cold Cornwall in the winter of 1970, he was a friendly, funny guy, carefree in his lifestyle but intense in his work. He was making *Straw Dogs* (1971).

I was making a profile of him for BBC television and he couldn't have been more co-operative. In the posh Tregenna Castle Hotel where we were all staying, he was full of jokes and pranks. One evening, to the amazement of the diners, he jumped onto the table and called out: 'Ever see an Eskimo pee?', with which he unzipped his flies and a cascade of ice cubes fell onto the floor. He was different from any actor I had met before, ever watchful of those around him. When we finished our documentary and there was a meal back at the hotel, at the end of the evening he came up to me and said: 'Do you realise that when you were filming me you would look into my eyes and nod wisely at everything I said but tonight you didn't pay any attention to me at all?' I think it was a sort of compliment.

The next time we met he was in a very different mood. It was in even colder Yorkshire, where he was making Kathleen Tynan's *Agatha* (1979) – a fictionalised account of the 11 days when Agatha Christie went missing in 1926. Hoffman was playing what had been the small part of Wally Stanton, an American journalist who tracks her down. But First Artists insisted he be a co-lead with Vanessa Redgrave, so Arthur Hopcraft and Murray Schisgal had been brought in to pump up his part.

I asked him how he was and Hoffman replied: 'I'm fulfilling my contract with First Artists and then I'm going to get the fuck out of here. I literally got down on my knees and begged them not to start the film. The script's being rewritten every day. It's every actor's nightmare, it's painting a picture on railroad tracks with the train getting closer. It's crazy time.'

Hoffman became embroiled in a long litigation with First Artists and found himself in some more: his wife, Anne, was suing him for divorce. So he was not in the best of humour when Robert Benton and Stanley Jaffe flew in to persuade him to play Kramer. In fact, he had vowed to himself never to make another film, but to return to the stage.

Kramer vs. Kramer matters in understanding Streep not just because of her acting but because of a defining moment that showed how her confidence was growing.

Both Benton and Jaffe had made their mark in cinema – Benton had written *Bonnie and Clyde* (1967) and Jaffe had produced *Goodbye Columbus* (1969). Both agreed that Hoffman was the only man to play Kramer. They had sent him a copy of Avery Corman's best-selling novel in advance, but he had found it more 'contrived' than he hoped. And he wasn't too keen on Benton's screenplay and he didn't like the part as it was written. 'Can we agree that the script is crap and begin again?' he said to Benton.

If I had been the double Oscar-nominated screenwriter who had once opined: 'I always thought the actors were hired to ruin the writer's lines,' my inclination would have been to bid Hoffman farewell and jump on the next Concorde back home. But the kindly Benton agreed to Hoffman's suggestion that they work together on the script. In fact, he had a cunning plan. He could see how he could incorporate the character of Dustin Hoffman into that of Jack Kramer and come up with an alloy that was stronger than either of them. For the record Hoffman did concede: 'It's not a piece of crap but can we treat it that way so that we're quite tough?'

They spent several weeks with a tape-recorder in New York's Carlyle Hotel and – despite Benton's writer friends saying to him 'Oh, you poor thing!' – the experiment worked. Benton later said: 'If the film's got any truth in it, that's as much to do with Dustin as with me.' The star responded: 'I'd turn to Benton and would say "I've got an idea". And this smile would come on his face. I've never seen that in so many years. I'd say that to other directors and they would get green – I'd think they were going to throw up. The worst thing you can say to most directors is "I've got an idea."'

The plot remained much the same: Joanna Kramer, after eight years of marriage, leaves her husband, Ted, and five-year-old son, Billy, as she feels she needs to find herself. Eighteen months later she has done so, and returns to New York to claim custody of the child. In the interim Ted has become both father and mother to Billy and formed a bond that wasn't there when the child's mother was. Joanna's departure, Stanley Jaffe the producer said, is 'the most heinous thing a woman can do '- well, that's arguable – but what is less so is why he cast Streep: 'Joanna has to be inherently likeable. Meryl has the best face of anybody on the screen, intelligence and goodness come out of her.'

I made the mistake of suggesting to Streep that maybe Joanna was a bit ruthless and uncaring for leaving her child.

'Are you crazy?' she snapped back. 'I don't believe that. She was a little nuts, neurotic and very weak. So what should she do? Take him in a backpack across country if she doesn't know where she's going? She doesn't have any money – in that kind of marriage the man controls the bank account. The little boy goes to school. He has his own life, his own bed. That's important. I don't think she's even going to live. I think she was suicidal – at least, that's what she said. I don't think you bring your child along on a suicide mission.'

There was a continuing key to Streep's choice of film parts at this time. On the stage, in Shakespeare or other well-established playwrights, she was prepared to play a person who was evil or, at least, of dubious morality. But rarely on the screen.

We owe to Streep the theory that the actor is an advocate. She said: 'If there's any thread that runs through my characters, it is that I have had a relationship with them where I have had to defend them. I thought that Joanna Kramer was not in a maze. She had no choice. Sick people very often don't have a choice and I thought she was mentally ill, depressed, out of control. She knew her life lay on the other side of the gang-plank. She had to get off that ship and she didn't know how it was going to turn out. Also, I knew I had the chance to come back at the end and explain who this terribly imploded person was.'

The body of the film consists of Ted building up his tender relationship with Billy (Justin Henry) but the crescendo is when Joanna returns to reclaim him. She has been to California where she has found a job, a shrink and, eventually, her missing self-esteem. She meets Ted in a Manhattan restaurant and informs him she has been back in New York for two months, is employed and would like custody of Billy. Ted fumes with indignation at the very suggestion.

When they had done several takes of the restaurant scene, Hoffman felt this wasn't coming across. He took the cameraman, Nestor Almendros, to one side and, in a whisper, asked him to open up the shot a little so the wall behind where he was sitting was clearly visible. Then he asked Benton for another take. In this one, when he rose to leave in anger, he swiped his glass of white wine with the back of his hand so that it hit the wall and shattered. The shock in Streep's reaction is palpable on screen.

She was not greatly pleased by the improvisation. 'Next time you do that, I'd appreciate you letting me know,' she coolly informed him. Today there is a framed photograph of the two of them on the wall next to the table at JG Melon's on 74th and 3rd where the scene was shot.

Streep got revenge of a sort. She told me that, in the battle of Hoffman vs Streep, when it came to the court room scene at the end of the film, where the parents do battle for custody of Billy: 'They felt they had a great movie but in that scene they didn't know what to do. They didn't have an argument for her when she goes on the stand, they didn't know what her point of view should be. I said "Are you kidding? She was the mother for five and a half years. Just because you've shown him being the mother for eighteen months –

big deal! You know she has some rights here." It didn't seem confusing to me. I know I wouldn't give up my baby that easily.'

So Benton suggested to her that maybe she should write a draft of her testimony. This she duly did, quite quickly, on a flight back from Indianapolis, where she and Don had been visiting his parents. On the day of shooting she handed it to Benton – who had temporarily forgotten he had asked her to try this. He read it, thought it was perfect and told her he would shoot it all.

But they didn't tell Dustin Hoffman.

In the film Streep took the stand. This is what Joanna said: 'During the last five years of our marriage, I was becoming more and more unhappy, more troubled. I needed somebody to help me but when I turned to Ted he wasn't there for me so we became more and more isolated from each other. Because of his attitude towards my fears and his inability to deal with my feelings, I had come to have almost no self-esteem. I was scared and unhappy and, in my mind, I had no other choice but to leave. In my mind I thought there was something terribly wrong with me and my son would be better off without me.'

Benton was delighted but 'Dustin was furious', Streep recalled with a chuckle. 'I could see the steam coming out of his ears because he hadn't been able to read it first, to know what I was going to say. It was really a fun day.'

At the very end of the film, when Joanna, having

won custody, arrives to tell Ted he can keep Billy after all, Streep scripted the compassionate line: 'I came here to take my son home but I realize he already is home.'

Hoffman said he wanted her to cry at that moment. 'I knew she wasn't over Johnny Cazale so I went over to her and said something to her about him.' It is doubtful if Streep needed such tricks. Unlike Dustin, she was in a happy marriage and, at the time, heavily pregnant with her first child which, she remarked, 'is a great way for an actress to get a close-up.'

I asked her what Hoffman was like. 'He's very energised,' she replied. 'The most wonderful combination of generous and selfish I've ever met, all wrapped up in one man. He really wants to be the greatest actor that ever lived. But he's a smart actor and a good actor and he knows you're only as good as the repartee. You both bring each other up. So he's torn the whole time. He wants you to be good – but he doesn't.'

Hoffman considered her 'an ox when it comes to acting. She eats work for breakfast. She keeps trying to hit the perfect ball.' He also confided in a post-film interview that there were times when he 'hated her guts.'

The phrase reached Streep's ears without being softened, that and other adverse remarks.

She confessed: 'I only found out much later when I was doing the publicity that he was mad at me. I still don't know why. I read in interviews that he was so furious with me and I was playing a game and it was like tennis with Pete Sampras, you've got to be on your game. I don't know how to play tennis and I wasn't in competition.'

I do not recall either of them turning up at the other's American Film Institute Life Achievement Awards. But they did turn up at the following April's Oscars where Benton won a brace for writing and directing, Hoffman won Best Actor and Streep Best Supporting Actress – possibly the only Supporting Actress whose character's name was in the film's title. Her screen time has been calculated at less that fifteen minutes, but those fifteen minutes brought her fame and fortune and established her as one of the country's leading screen actresses.

The film was not only a huge hit – it had quite an impact on American culture. For some years to follow, family court judges would cite the fictional *Kramer vs. Kramer* in matrimonial disputes almost as frequently as real legal precedents.

5

Sophie

Streep wanted very badly to play the title role in *Sophie's Choice* (1982). The only problem was that the director had already cast someone else.

William Styron maintained that the theme for his novel just popped into his head when he woke up on a beautiful spring day. 'I don't mean to say that when I had that particular inspiration that I saw the whole story,' he recalled. 'But I did see this particular moment – the choice.' This was the secret that Sophie guards for most of the book. She is taken to Auschwitz with her two children. A drunken German, a young doctor, asks her which of her children she wants to save. She prevaricates, saying she is a Pole and a Christian. He tells her if she doesn't choose he will take both away. She gives him her daughter, Eva, on the grounds that she will be stronger than her son, Jan. In the event neither survive.

Stryon's masterstroke was to grapple with the question of absolute, personal guilt. The German doctor at Auschwitz was no longer the conduit of evil; he was the author of evil. Hannah Arendt, the German philosopher, who coined the term 'the banality of evil', said that the only answer to the question: 'Where was God at Auschwitz?' was 'Where was man?' Styron rationalized that the doctor, 'by committing the most intolerable sin that he was able to conceive' was trying to restore his belief in God in a Godless place.

The film could not go too far down this complex route but Styron professed he was pleased with Pakula's screenplay – 'It could have been melodramatic or trivialised' – while saying he had no wish to write it – 'One gets stale enough writing the work itself.'

Styron's daughter, Alexandra, wrote in *The New Yorker*: 'Sophie had come to him in a dream, Daddy always said. Not much older than I am now, he had woken up in Connecticut and been unable to shake the image of a woman he once knew. She'd lived above him in Flatbush, in the boarding house he immortalized as Yetta Zimmerman's Pink Palace. She was a Holocaust survivor, as evidenced by her wrist tattoo, Polish and beautiful, but more than that he didn't know. Her boyfriend was American, but undistinguished.'

Sophie has to invent a part to protect herself in post-war America, or she would go mad. She even praises her father who, in fact, was a strong advocate of the Holocaust. Styron – who died in 2006 – revealed in a late interview that like his narrator Stingo when Sophie started to talk about her father: 'I initially believed … that she was telling the truth about how wonderful he was. When I got further into the book, it occurred to me that she was really lying. I didn't realise it at first, which is a perfect example of a character taking over your imagination.'

One can imagine Streep reading the book when it came out in 1979 and knowing that, if she never played another part in her life, she just had to tackle this one.

There is an axiom in the film industry that great books do not tend to make great films, and it's generally true. Of course exceptions like *Dr Zhivago* and *Gone With The Wind* are there to prove the rule and *Sophie's Choice* joins this honourable pantheon. Styron realised that to compress the 632 pages of his novel, let alone the thoughts and philosophy contained therein, was a near-impossible task, but found that Pakula's script 'adhered to the spirit of the book.'

Stingo/Styron (played by the Texan Peter MacNicol who went on to a solid career in films and television but never again reached such dreamy heights) arrives at a boarding house, The Pink Palace, in Brooklyn to write the great novel. This is 1947. Already there, living above him, shaking his candelabra with their love-making and their fights, are Nathan Landau (Kline) and Sophie Zawistowski (Streep). They invite Stingo into their heady world: drinking and dancing and dressing in fancy clothes to go to Coney Island.

But here's the central irony. Whereas Stingo is sitting at his desk creating fiction, Nathan and Sophie *are* fiction. Nathan is not the great research biologist on the verge of a breakthrough for a polio cure as he would have us believe; just a failed science student. He is Jewish with an obsession about the Holocaust, his room stacked with books, papers and photographs relating to it. And now he has a living artefact, Sophie, who survived Auschwitz, a true victim.

But Sophie is an unreliable narrator of her core story. Endlessly she talks of her heroic and loving father, a professor who gave so much help to the Jews in Nazi-occupied Cracow – 'My father was a civilised man living in an uncivilised time.' Stingo is to learn that precisely the reverse was the case: her father was a rabid anti-semite who did everything in his power to incite his fellow Poles to help the Germans in the Final Solution. Stingo will also learn from Nathan's brother that his new friend is a paranoid schizophrenic whose lapses into unhinged anger take place when he fails to take his medication.

Nathan, in one of his rages, asks how Sophie, a non-Jew, was sent to Auschwitz. She says it was for stealing a ham to feed her children – and that five million non-Jews died in the camps.

In flashback we see how Nathan met Sophie when she collapsed in the atrium of a library. His doctor brother diagnosed anaemia and Nathan nursed her back to health, putting iron back into her body with liver, spinach and ferrous sulphate. 'Thank you for making me to bloom like a rose,' she says.

Also in flashback – in black and white – we go back to Auschwitz where Sophie, because of her command of languages – including German – goes to work as a secretary for the Camp Commandant, Hoess. She narrowly escapes being raped by him.

After reading the book in galleys, Pakula got a friend,

Keith Barrish, to put up the $750,000 to buy the film rights. He subsequently bumped into Styron at a party and told him: 'I hope I can do it.' Styron was worried and confided to his agent 'I hope he *can* do it.' Initial attempts at raising the budget from the studios were pretty disastrous. 'Double suicides are not the easiest thing to get financed,' Pakula drily recalled.

Fortunately an Englishman, Lew Grade, unfairly known in *Private Eye* as 'Low Greed', having made many millions in television, had decided to diversify into films to take on the might of the Hollywood studios. Things started well with *The Great Muppet Caper* (1981), using Jim Henson's original stars, Miss Piggy and Kermit the Frog. 'The good thing with Muppets,' Lew told me, 'is, unlike real actors, you don't have to pay them residuals.' He took a bit of a dip with his next venture *Raise the Titanic* (1981) which they shot in a specially constructed tank in Malta. Grade, memorably, observed: 'It would have been cheaper to lower the Atlantic.'

But Grade and his head of film, Martin Starger, liked the notion of *Sophie's Choice*. 'It won't be an easy motion picture with mass appeal,' Grade observed as he wrote Pakula a cheque for $12 million, 'but it might be an important one.'

Robert Brustein, the Dean of Yale Drama School, alerted the producers to the undoubted fact that Streep was right for Sophie. Pakula was keen to hire her and offered a deal.

Streep told me: 'I was making *The French Lieutenant's*

Woman in England and he called me up and said 'Have you read this book, *Sophie's Choice*? And I said 'Oh, yes'- I had read it some years ago. He then said 'I'm prepared to offer you the lead role in the film version.' I said 'Are you kidding?' He wasn't but he suggested I might want to read it again and I said 'Just send me the script.' He said he couldn't show it to anyone yet. So I said, 'What are you talking about? You want me to play this big part and I can't read it?' He drove me crazy and I think I drove him crazy. He said 'You have to know that since I can't be sure you'll do it, I have to also look at other actresses.'

Which he did many times.

Pakula considered Hanna Schygulla whose international star was riding high in television's *Berlin Alexanderplatz*, Marthe Keller, the Swiss actress who had made her mark opposite Dustin Hoffman in *Marathon Man*, and even Liv Ullman. But, at 42, she was too old for the romance with Nathan. It was even said that Goldie Hawn was keen to play the part – although her talent as a tragedian was, as yet, untested – and Barbra Streisand was prepared to play Sophie for no money, just a percentage of the profits. What profits there might have been if the end result had been Streisand playing a scrawny, blonde Polish girl is open to question.

Initially, Pakula was set on Magda Vasaryova, a Slovakian actress who had never made a film in English (and never would). Was it her performance as Rusalka, the water nymph, that drew her to him? She did six auditions. By the end of the last one he was convinced enough to sign her on. At the same time he had completed a shooting script – which Streep saw.

'About a year later I was able to get hold of a copy of the script through a secretary who was not meant to let anybody see it,' she told me conspiratorially. 'I read it and I thought 'you have just sent your career down the tubes'. It was the best part I'd read in ages and also a wonderful script.'

At this point her agent, Sam Cohn, took over. He telephoned Pakula and said: 'Meryl is too embarrassed to call you because you didn't send her a script. She knows you're not interested in her anymore. But she's sneaked a script and wants to play it.'

Reluctantly Pakula agreed to see Streep. 'I went to his office,' she recalled, 'and the four walls were covered with pictures of this beautiful Czech actress. And my heart just went down to my feet and I thought 'That's it!' But then I reasoned 'she's too young to play it – and too beautiful'. We talked and finally he agreed to see me again, and the next time we talked for three hours, and for the next two weeks I sat with my hand on the telephone until it rang and he said the part was mine.'

Pakula was also influenced by his producer, Martin Starger, who didn't think Magda could do the part. 'It was very clear she had a lot of problems with her English. I said to Alan 'This is a very difficult film on a very difficult subject without you making it more difficult. Magda doesn't speak the language, you should reconsider Meryl.'

71

Magda recovered from her disappointment and took to Real Life becoming an ambassador for the Republic of Slovakia and even standing for President.

Streep was delighted. The story mattered a lot to her. 'When I was ten I opened a book at the library and there were photographs of the Lebensraum programme where children were taken away, supposedly to be adopted. But they were abandoned and they starved and died. The Allies arrived and saw the piled up bodies in the back of the trucks. I will never forget that image. It formed the basis of my emotional understanding of unimaginable horror.'

Before she heard she had the part, Streep told Pakula: 'Regardless of who plays Sophie, there's only one actor who's right for Nathan and that's Kevin Kline.' She had known him since they were both disciples of Joe Papp. In February 1978, Hal Prince had cast Kline as Madeline Kahn's lover in the musical *On the Twentieth Century* and Kline had won a Tony. He was an accomplished musician and singer, having studied at the Julliard School and became the toast of New York for his performance as the Pirate King in *The Pirates of Penzance* which Papp produced and Wilfred Leach directed. It started out as a Public Theater production in Central Park but became a Broadway phenomenon.

The rock stars Linda Ronstadt and Rex Smith, as the young lovers, were cast as the bait to get people into the Uris Theater – but word of mouth soon centered on Kline. Having grown up on tedious school productions, I personally found Gilbert and Sullivan an ersatz entertainment, neither opera nor musical. But when I saw Kline my attitude altered: he was mesmeric, prancing round the stage, stealing the conductor's baton to use as a sword, a human bolt of lightning.

Frank Rich, the theatre critic of *The New York Times*, agreed. 'Mr Kline is in a class by himself,' he wrote. 'He has all the ingredients for conventional leading-man stardom – a big voice, dashing good looks, infinite charm – and yet he's also blessed with the grace and timing of a silent-movie clown. As the Pirate King, he can show off all his gifts. He flies from the stage to the ramp in a single bound; he coddles any woman who isn't nailed down; he engages in sword fights with half the chorus as well as any inanimate objects that cross his path. And then there are those perfect pratfalls: Mr Kline tumbles from lofty perches only to bounce up in a flash, deadpan and demented, for still more comic punishment. One must wonder how long "Pirates" – or anything – will be able to keep this performer in captivity.'

Kevin has since become a friend – I worked with him on *A Fish Called Wanda* (1988) and *Fierce Creatures* (1987) which I co-wrote with John Cleese, in which we created three parts for Kevin: Vince the marketing man, Rod, his Murdoch-like father and Muriel, his mother (the last was shot but, wrongly as far as I was concerned, not shown). Kevin has never ceased to amaze me with his improvisation, his interpretation and his invention. In many ways, he is the nearest male equivalent of

73

Streep and being with him on set is like attending a master class in acting.

But, in 1979, he had never made a movie. He devoured *Sophie's Choice* and a fellow actor said to him: 'I just read this fantastic book which is going to make a great movie. Nathan would be a perfect part for you but they'll probably get some movie star to play it.'

It is greatly to Pakula's credit that he took the risk. He observed that Kline was 'a movie star in the classic sense' and he had the confidence to cast him. Pakula knew that he had to find a man who could do melting charm, frenetic energy and psychotic danger.

Peter MacNicol, quite simply, came along and auditioned with many others for Stingo. He was the last person they saw. MacNicol was playing the small (12 minutes on stage) part of a Southern lawyer in the Manhattan Theatre Club's production of Beth Henley's *Crimes of the Heart* when Alixe Gordon, Pakula's casting director, spotted him. Maybe it wasn't the strongest piece of casting – Stingo is Styron who was a tall man with film star looks, and MacNicol isn't. So the fact that he sleeps with Sophie and intends to take her home to the South to marry her is not the most plausible part of the movie.

The film is, in essence, a very small ensemble piece – there are only three significant people in it – about an enormous, heart-rending topic. Pakula rehearsed the trio for four weeks, advising Streep: 'This is the story of a woman who has no heroism in her, the story of a girl who has no courage. It's her terrible problem and you're just the opposite of that. There is an open sensuality about this woman in her relationship with Nathan and you are a very dignified woman.'

'And an actress,' Streep might have reminded him. She and Kevin came up with a tempestuous, haunting relationship; they both sense, like mayflies, that their time on earth is limited so they must live their lives to the full. 'Once we sat down at a piano that was part of the set for Sophie's room,' Kevin recalled, 'we suddenly found ourselves in the middle of an impromptu jam session that turned out to be the ideal ending for the scene we were working on.' It helped that Kline is a pianist of professional standards and was able to turn Beethoven into ragtime with a flick of his wrists.

Kevin would sometimes sleep overnight on the set. 'I wanted to know what it is like to be locked up in that place and have to create a life of the imagination as I have no life outside.' Kevin, more than any other actor I've observed, needs to live inside the body of his character. Once, on Wanda, he came up to the director, Charles Crichton, and asked him what time of day a certain scene was meant to be taking place. There was no particular time – it was just a random scene – but Charlie told him it was early afternoon and Kevin, satisfied, walked away with the words 'I wonder what Otto would have had for lunch.'

Kevin was relieved that Pakula shot the film in sequence so that he could nuance Nathan's decline into his final madness and suicide. Streep was equally impressed by Pakula. 'Some directors take jobs and they think 'This will be a commercial hit.' Or they work to answer and confound their critics. But Alan did work that fed his soul and sought to answer all the endless questions of life.'

They filmed in New York at Manhattan's Camera Mart Studios, while in Brooklyn a large grey mansion on Rugby Road was painted to become The Pink Palace where the three live. Pakula's attempt to use Brooklyn Bridge as some kind of metaphor for a chance for freedom didn't really work.

Naturally some chief at Universal Pictures suggested that the joint suicide of Sophie and Nathan at the end of the film would be bad box office and perhaps they could live happily ever after? Streep and Kline soon knocked that notion on the head. Instead Stingo finds the dead lovers entwined in each other's arms and, in Shakespearean fashion, recites Emily Dickinson's poem over them:

Ample make this bed,
Make this bed with awe,
In it wait till judgement break
Excellent and fair.

Kline commented at the New York wrap: 'The experience of *Sophie's Choice* was the most wonderful acting experience I have ever had or am ever likely to have.'

It was left to Streep to shoot the Auschwitz sequences. There had been rumbles that budget problems would force them to do those in New York but she resolutely refused. Unlike *Holocaust*, when she couldn't wait to come home, here she knew she needed a place that would give the dank horror of the camp and it was built in Zagreb in what was then Yugoslavia.

In the pivotal scene where Sophie gives up her daughter, Streep recalled: 'I thought I would be crying but when it came what happened was this silent scream.' She could never open Styron's book again.

She had given a performance of operatic power and heart-rending pathos and duly won the Academy Award for Best Actress. It was her fourth trip to the ceremony. 'It's a lot of fun for your parents,' she told me. 'My mother gets all dressed up and my father wears a tuxedo. The first time my mother had Gregory Peck sitting in front of her and Jimmy Stewart breathing down her neck. Normally nothing bothers her, but she was trembling. I can make a multi-million dollar film without it worrying me but at that ceremony I get so terribly nervous. Once I came out in hives and another time I was wearing a beautiful, purple silk dress with great circles of sweat under the arms. That set-up is just guaranteed to give you an ulcer.'

When Sylvester Stallone read out her name as winner, she embraced her husband Don and, as she mounted the stage, dropped her acceptance speech. Streep told the audience: 'You can't imagine what this is like – so incredibly thrilling right down to your toes. I have a lot of people to thank and I'm going to be one of those people who tries to mention a lot of names, because I know that just two seconds ago my mother and father went berserk and I'd like to give some other mothers and fathers the same opportunity.' And so she did for the next two minutes, then looked at her statuette. 'I feel I owe this to Kevin Kline and Peter MacNicol because everything I had, I got from looking in their eyes.'

Her nerves did not disappear after she left the stage but her statuette nearly did. She went to the bathroom off the retiring area and, as she prepared to meet the press, she heard a shout of 'My God, somebody's left an Oscar in the ladies!'

It was Streep's.

6

Nuclear Fallout

May 1977.

James Callaghan was Prime Minister. Mrs Thatcher, the new Leader of the Opposition, was considered a liability to the Tories. I was in the BBC canteen trying to digest what passed for lunch at the BBC's Lime Grove Studios. These were the sound stages where Alfred Hitchcock had shot *The Man Who Knew Too Much* (1934) and *The 39 Steps* (1935).

A tall girl with blonde hair, smartly dressed in a cream two-piece suit, and carrying a tray, stood beside us.

'Mind if I join you?' she asked.

We made some room for Margaret Jay.

'You look a bit down,' somebody said to her.

'I am,' she replied. 'Peter's going to Washington.'

'For The Times?' I asked. Her husband was the paper's Economics Editor.

Margaret shook her head. 'As Ambassador. David Owen thinks he'll get on well with Jimmy Carter.' David Owen was the Foreign Secretary then and Margaret's father was Prime Minister so her husband's appointment led to charges of nepotism.

Jimmy Carter was the first US President to have some knowledge of nuclear technology. On his watch he responded well to the accident at Three Mile Island when a nuclear plant nearly went critical. Streep was not then very vocal about nuclear issues but that was to change soon – thanks to Nora Ephron.

Nora Ephron first worked on newspapers and then gained a reputation as a magazine journalist. She heard about Karen Silkwood, a union activist who died in mysterious circumstances in November 1974 when she was about to meet a *New York Times* reporter and blow the whistle on acts of negligence at a plutonium plant.

Silkwood's death attracted national attention: an article in *Ms.* magazine and, in 1981, a book *The Killing of Karen Silkwood: The Story Behind The Kerr-McGee Plutonium Case* by Richard Rashke. When ABC Motion Pictures saw the film potential, they knew the story needed to be approached from a woman's point of view, so who better than the wife of the famous Watergate investigator, Carl Bernstein. Ephron wrote the original screenplay with fellow journalist, Alice Arlen. No actress was hotter at the time than Meryl Streep, with an Oscar for *Kramer vs. Kramer.* Her agent, Sam Cohn, liked to package projects and knew that another star client, Mike Nichols, was anxious to return to directing mainstream cinema, and equally anxious to work with Streep. Theirs was to prove the most fruitful continuing partnership of her career.

Nichols had already heard about Streep from a fellow director, Arvin Brown, who ran The Long Wharf Theatre.

'He (Arvin Brown) told me that when he directed her in *27 Wagon Loads of Cotton*, she said to him after about ten days or two weeks of rehearsal, 'If I don't find my character by the end of this week I'm going to quit, I'm not going to do this, because I've gone on too long and haven't found her.' Then she found some big thatched dress, she became fat in it and was completely transformed, found her character, and that was that. I asked him 'Who is this person?' And he said 'Well, you'll work with her. Her name is Meryl Streep, and there's no question – there was never a question – of Meryl ever looking for a job.'

Nichols (original name Michael Igor Peschkowsky) had been born in Berlin in 1931. He and his family fled Germany to escape the Nazis in 1939, and settled in Chicago. He arrived with no English and no hair as he suffered from alopecia. Being a bald German during the war was not a guarantee of popularity at school. One does not have to be Freud to work out why he escaped into comedy. While studying at the University of Chicago in the 1950s, Nichols met Elaine May.

Elaine Berlin (as she was then) was born in Philadelphia in 1932, the daughter of theatre director and actor. As a child, she occasionally performed with her father in the Yiddish theatre he ran.

For both Nichols and May, the pivotal event of their careers was their chance encounter in the spring of 1954. Nichols said: 'My first impression of her was of a beautiful and dangerous girl who interested me enormously, and scared me. We were both what was known on campus as "dangerous". We were introduced, and then we oddly met again in the railway station on the way back to the South Side of Chicago, where the university was.

'I said: "May I sit down?"

'She said: "Eeef you wish."

'And just like that, we started to improvise – we did a whole long spy mystery improvisation for the benefit of the other people on the bench. That's how we met ... and then we were friends. We did it later on one of the records, but we improvised it in the actual railroad station the first time, before we knew each other.'

It was Lennon meeting McCartney. Nichols and May's brilliant double act, which satirised contemporary social issues and, especially partnership problems, hit Broadway in 1960. After they split in 1961, Nichols turned to directing. It seemed he could not put a foot wrong with a succession of Neil Simon hit comedies, *Barefoot in the Park* (1963), *The Odd Couple* (1965), and *Plaza Suite* (1968).

Nichols' film directing debut, Edward Albee's *Who's Afraid of Virginia Woolf?* (1966) with Elizabeth Taylor and Richard Burton, continued his charmed life. (During filming, Nichols later confessed to our mutual friend, the late Gordon Arnell, that Elizabeth Taylor noticed the problems he had with his wig and put him on to her hairdresser – who solved the problem for good.) 'Virginia Woolf' had been two hours of marital madness but Nichols' gift for dry humour was never better displayed than in *The Graduate* (1967), which won him

82

an Oscar for Best Director. Nichols once told me there was a strong 'water metaphor' running through it is something I have, as yet, been unable to divine.

But, as Chaucer said, 'all good things must come to an end'. *Catch 22* (1970) and *Carnal Knowledge* (1972) were good – but not as good as it can get. Nichols' nemesis came in 1975 with *The Fortune*. The makers formed the sort of dream team that couldn't go wrong: Jack Nicholson and Warren Beatty as buddy-adversaries, a script from Carol Eastman, who had done so well with Nicholson in *Five Easy Pieces* (1970), and Nichols himself. But it did go wrong. 'The danger of comedy is that it is a binary art form: people either laugh or they don't,' Kevin Kline once pointed out to me. And, in this instance, they didn't. So Nichols gave up the movies and returned to producing television and theatre.

Until he met Streep, comedy was what he excelled at and so did she, so it was natural that a comedy was what they should film together. He tried to get the rights to *Private Lives* – the play Noel Coward wrote for himself and Gertrude Lawrence. It had been filmed in 1931 with Robert Montgomery and Norma Shearer, and was ripe for a revival. But the Coward Estate preferred a stage version with Richard Burton and Elizabeth Taylor.

Silkwood could not have been more diametrically different. Karen Silkwood studied medical technology at university and then got a job as a chemical technician at the Kerr-McGee Plutonium Fuels Production Plant in Crescent, Oklahoma. There she became a member of the Oil, Chemical and Atomic Workers Union. She was 26 and was soon intent on exposing safety lapses. She even found that she was the victim of a number of unexplained exposures to plutonium and was about to reveal all this to the *New York Times* reporter but, while driving to their rendezvous, crashed and died. The incriminating documents she was taking to this meeting were never found. What police did find were alcohol and Quaaludes in her system – and also the possibility that her car might have been hit from behind in what was an otherwise inexplicable accident.

Streep played Karen Silkwood as a louche, gum-chewing working girl with a what-the-hell attitude to profanities, drink, drugs and sex. Streep recalls: 'I was attracted to the character. No matter what I think in my real life, in order to effectively play a part or make my imagination go, I have to be presented with a certain challenge and a character with problems. What I liked about Karen was that she wasn't Joan of Arc at all. She was unsavoury in some ways and, yet, she did some very good things.'

Streep even went as far as to break her self imposed 'no nudity', and gave a quick flash of a breast to some heckling male workers at the plant because it was the sort of thing she felt Karen might do spontaneously.

None of the principle players signed up for the movie for political motives. Streep said, 'This doesn't feel like an anti-nuclear movie. There are lots of those around, and I've stayed away from them quite purposefully because I don't like polemics. I think everybody should talk all the time about what they believe. There's not enough political talk in this country. This film is more complicated, it seems to me, and even-handed in a funny, real-life way. The people on both sides of the question are all pretty recognizable. It has the feeling of real working life, and I think it's about that more than anything nuclear.'

In the film Karen shares a house with her boyfriend, Drew (Kurt Russell), and a lesbian friend, Dolly, played by Cher – whose main previous film appearance had been in *Wild on the Beach* (1965). Nichols knew, through his experience with Art Garfunkel, the co-lead with Jack Nicholson in *Carnal Knowledge*, that certain pop performers can bring a fresh, natural quality to the screen. And this Cher did.

Both Russell and Cher met the people they were playing. Streep was, of course, unable to. 'All I had were pieces of information from different sources. I had details from five or six people that all described a different woman. It made me think I really ought to write my autobiography before I go, because once you're gone, everybody has a different version of you.'

Although *Silkwood* was apparently a 1960s film dealing with corporate corruption, political activism, class and gender, the film was, at its core, a character study about a woman and her friendships.

Streep came on to the film almost straight from shooting the most harrowing Auschwitz sequences in *Sophie's Choice*.

'Mike spoke of the film as being about people who

are asleep in their lives, then waking up: 'How did I get here?' And that's exactly how I felt. One day I was in Yugoslavia and the next I found myself in a plant with a light flashing and a siren going, 'Whoop whoop whoop,' thinking 'How did this happen?"'

Nichols observed that Streep's greatest strength was her ability to transform herself into another person. 'When we were shooting *Silkwood*, I saw a screening of *Sophie's Choice* and I was stunned because I thought we were filming the real Meryl, but the person on the screen in *Sophie's Choice* was *also* the real Meryl. I will never get used to it.'

Streep herself finds this metamorphosis difficult to articulate. Part of it she attributes to Nichols who, she says: 'Makes the soup and pours all the ingredients in. I'm just one of them.' The rest remains an elusive struggle. 'I always start a film at Point A and I feel I'm without resource or imagination. I think: maybe I should take notes, or maybe I should find a method. But since it's such a mysterious process – making movies, making a character – people imagine that you may have many more secrets and tricks and methods than you really do. The best actors start blank.'

Meryl, Cher, Mike, Nora and Alice were all nominated for Oscars, and Cher won a Golden Globe for Best Performance by an Actress in a Supporting Role in a Motion Picture.

Vincent Canby, the Film Critic of *The New York Times*, had high praise for Nichols. 'Though far from perfect, *Silkwood* may be the most serious work Mr Nichols has yet done in films, and that would include *Who's Afraid of Virginia Woolf?*, *The Graduate*, and *Catch-22*. Perhaps for the first time in a popular movie has America's petrochemical-nuclear landscape been dramatized, and with such anger and compassion.'

He went on: 'Miss Streep looks to be on what the Las Vegas people call 'a roll'. Her portrait of the initially self-assured and free-living, then radicalized and, finally, terrified, Karen Silkwood is unlike anything she has done to date, except in its intelligence. It's a brassy, profane, gum-chewing tour de force, as funny as it is moving.'

She had accomplished the 'tragical-historical'; now it was time to move on to the 'comical–romantical–sexual–political'.

Peter Jay's appointment to Washington caused some controversy as his wife's father was the Prime Minister. The Foreign Office had to ease out the incumbent Ambassador in Washington, Sir Peter Ramsbotham, to a job he didn't want, Governor of Bermuda. I met him at a dinner subsequently, and he told me how miffed he had felt.

Once in Washington, Peter and Margaret Jay became friends with Carl Bernstein who, along with Bob Woodward, had exposed President Nixon's complicity in the Watergate break-in, an attempted bugging by the wonderfully-named 'plumbers', to try and get hold of some Democratic party election tactics. Possibly unwisely in hindsight, Margaret and Carl became too friendly and, in 1980, had an affair. This enraged Carl's wife, Nora Ephron, the more so as she was pregnant with their second son.

True to the maxim, revenge is a dish best eaten cold, three years after she and Carl Bernstein split up, Ephron took the facts out of the ice-box and mixed them into a thinly-disguised *roman à clef* called *Heartburn*. It was cruel about the Margaret Jay character, saying that she looked like a giraffe with big feet. It was also cruel about the nature of Carl's alleged sex addiction, asserting he was 'capable of having sex with a Venetian blind.'

In a town as litigious as Washington it was improbable that Nora Ephron would retell things exactly as they were. The novel is ostensibly about Mark, a syndicated Washington columnist, and Rachel, a food writer who appears on TV – a middlebrow Julia Child crossed with a highbrow Dinah Shore (of whom earlier). When Rachel is seven months pregnant she discovers Mark has been having an affair with Thelma, the wife of an Under-Secretary of State, Jonathan Rice. Ephron knew her political territory; she had been a White House intern during the presidency of JFK.

Ephron's poisoned arrows flew straight into their targets. Thelma/Margaret has 'a neck as long as an arm and a nose as long as a thumb and you should see her legs, never mind her feet, which are sort of splayed.' And Jonathan/Peter Jay doesn't escape either. 'If I'd spent nineteen years with Jonathan Rice, I would have run off with a delivery boy from the Fleet Messenger Service.'

When Rachel becomes a born-again single, a man looks at her invitingly on the underground train. 'I wondered whether he was single, and if so, whether he was a college graduate and straight. Then I thought how awful it would be to be single again, how awful to be back on the market with the old New York ratio going against me – two hundred single women to every straight single man – packs of Amazons roaming the streets looking in vain for someone genuinely eligible and self-supporting who didn't mind a little cellulite.'

Rachel's marriage has come to an end not with a whimper but a bang as – the final evidence having been established by Mark's credit card and telephone details – she throws a Key lime pie at him when they are dining with friends. There is a certain dramatic irony in the food analogy as Rachel has threaded recipes throughout the novel, even giving us a recipe index at the end.

The book was a best seller and the film rights were snapped up by Paramount. Who better to adapt it for the movies than Ephron herself? She had been nominated for an Oscar for her screenplay of *Silkwood* (1983). Who better to play 'her' on the screen than Streep? She had also been nominated for an Oscar for that film and had befriended Nora. Who better to direct than Mike Nichols? He had also been nominated for his directing on the same project. And who better to play Mark/Carl than Dustin Hoffman? He had already played Carl Bernstein in *All the President's Men* (1976).

Well, no. Not the last. There was another, unseen. writer on the screenplay of *Heartburn*, namely Carl Bernstein's lawyer, and while he might have let Nora wash his client's dirty linen in public with the book, the thought of suing Paramount and its owner, Gulf and Western Industries, for a multi-million sum for defamation must have been very appealing. It certainly caused the script to be nudged further and further away from Ephron's real life story and, her first fictional version of it.

Hoffman, having already played Carl, was a little too close for comfort, so producer Robert Greenhut, who had produced Woody Allen's films, went for the third best-known Jewish star, Mandy Patinkin, who had played Tateh in *Ragtime* (1981), and Paul, the brother, in *Daniel* (1983) – the film about the nuclear spies the Rosenbergs – and was currently hot, having just been Barbra Streisand's love interest in *Yentl* (1983).

Mandy Patinkin agreed terms and shooting started. And then stopped. For some reason he left the film. Did he walk or was he pushed?

'Patinkin was removed from the film for being too intense and not funny enough,' pronounced the film and television reporter, Marshall Fine. Maybe he was right.

Mandy is not an easy man, as I found to my cost when I was making a TV profile of Barbra Streisand on the *Yentl* set. She was extremely popular with the cast and crew. But not with Mandy. He just didn't want to talk about her.

'I am difficult,' he has admitted – though not to me. 'No one is going to beat the crap out of me more than me.' Even Steven Sondheim, of whose musicals he is the supreme interpreter, says that he is 'meticulous to the point of madness.' Meticulous and maybe sensitive to what directors really want. After Mandy left *Heartburn*, he said: 'I think Mike Nichols always wanted Jack Nicholson.'

Nichols had directed Nicholson as the sex-obsessed lawyer in the Jules Feiffer film *Carnal Knowledge* (1971), so he knew he could empathise with the part of Mark. Nicholson, in turn, had long wanted to work with Streep. After Jane Fonda turned it down, he had considered her for the part of Julia, a character in *Goin' South* (1978) – a lugubrious comedy-western which he directed, but, instead, gave Mary Steenburgen her screen debut. And he and Bob Raphaelson had wanted Streep to play the part of Cora, the highly-sexed wife of a lunch wagon owner in James M. Cain's *The Postman Always Rings Twice* (1981), but Streep thought the role was too raunchy.

So Streep and Nicholson at last came together in *Heartburn*. She wore a short, dark wig and did a clever impression of the real Nora Ephron, but Nicholson kept his interpretation of the character far from anyone in any way resembling Carl Bernstein.

But now it looked like a marriage made in heaven. Mark and Rachel meet at a wedding and end up in bed. At four in the morning she cooks him spaghetti carbonara, remarking wittily: 'You probably think it very bourgeois to cook for someone on the first date.' Mark tells Rachel he wants carbonara once a week when they're married.

She says: 'I don't believe in marriage.'
He says: 'Neither do I.'

And then they marry – and from then on things go wrong.

The film is also notable for the debut of Kevin Spacey. He robs a group therapy session after giving up his seat to a pregnant Rachel. Much of the script, while funny, was less dialogue than monologue – more suitable for a stand-up routine. 'The most unfair thing about this whole business is that I can't even date,' Rachel broods. 'Who else would bother with me? There I was, seven months gone, swaybacked, awkward, bloated, logy, with a belly button that looked like a pumpkin stem and feet that felt like old cucumbers.'

Streep was pregnant when she made the film: ' I got pregnant in Africa. And I got really, really sick, with something African. So I look at *Heartburn* and all I can see is my green, green, green face.'

Nevertheless she certainly enjoyed her first screen engagement with Nicholson: 'At first it was scary. He terrified me. He was Jack Nicholson! I only became "emeritus" recently, and he'd been that for years.' It's telling Streep should use such an academic title; professors are 'emeritus', but not usually film stars.

Streep added: 'He was a force of nature, a friend of Mike's, and so I thought: "Is there going to be be room for me?" But there was. I just remember laughing all the time, he's very funny and incredibly witty and takes the piss out of everybody.'

Nicholson reciprocated: 'She's my idol. That rapport

was great and almost instant. There's nobody out there that far in the movies. Nobody. That's New Jersey, baby.'

Maybe Ephron was too close to the story, maybe Bernstein's lawyers were even closer ... but the undoubted talents of Nichols, Nicholson and Streep didn't manage to engage the audience. There were good moments: Rachel and Mark eating pizzas with trowels (Streep's idea) in their construction site of a house, and singing songs for their yet-to-arrive first baby. When Mark sings 'My Boy Bill' from Rodgers and Hammerstein's *Carousel*, it was a nice gesture to Nora's parents, Phoebe and Henry Ephron, who wrote the screenplay for the 1956 movie, and helped produce it. Streep's family also got a bit of work: her mother, Mary, and her brother, Dana, played dinner party guests, and her daughter, Mamie, played her daughter in the film.

Neither the critics nor the public had as much fun as the cast had had. Very mixed reviews greeted the film, and a paltry $25 million at the box-office. Roger Ebert wrote in *The Chicago Sun-Times*: 'Just by seeing their names on the marquee you'd figure the movie would have to be electrifying. But it's not. Here is the story of two people with no chemistry, played by two actors with great chemistry. The only way they can get into character is to play against the very things we like them for. Streep seems dowdy and querulous. Nicholson seems to be a shallow creep. Their romance never really seems real, never seems important and permanent. So

93

when he starts fooling around, we don't feel the enormity of the offense. There's not much in their marriage for him to betray.'

But the unlauded project did little to harm the careers of anyone involved, not least Nora Ephron who went on to write one of the best romantic comedies of recent times, *When Harry Met Sally* (1989). She also gave the wittiest speech of the evening at the 2004 American Film Institute tribute to Streep. 'I loved working with Meryl Streep. First I worked on *Silkwood* with her. Meryl played Karen Silkwood and then the Polish person and then the Danish person but the true stretch, if I do say so, was playing me in *Heartburn*. I highly recommend having Meryl Streep play you.'

By 2004, Nora Ephron evidently no longer felt constrained to deny Rachel was, indeed, her. She went on: 'If your husband is cheating on you with the car hop, get Meryl to play you – you will feel much better. If you get rear-ended in a parking lot, have Meryl play you. If a dingo eats your baby, call Meryl. She plays all of us better than we play ourselves. Although it's a little depressing to know that if you go to audition to play yourself, you would lose out to Meryl. Some days, when I'm having a hard day, I'll call up Meryl and she'll come and stand in for me. She's so good, people don't even notice. I call her at the end of the day and find out how I did and, inevitably, it's one of the best days I've ever had.'

7

Comic Relief

As she approached 40 (in 1989), Streep decided to immerse herself in a series of comedies. Two worked, two didn't – not a bad batting average in the cinema's trickiest genre. She started with a flop as Orion Pictures tried to convert the plump and popular ABC Television star, Rosanne Barr, from the small to the wide screen in *She-Devil* (1989).

The movie starts well. Barr, 200 lbs of New York prime rib, makes the worst of a bad job when it comes to her personal appearance. She is as in thrall to celebrity as any other suburban American housewife and, after accidentally splashing her Chardonnay on Streep's frock at a party, boasts at the bar: "I just spilled my wine on Mary Fisher, the famous author." '

But the famous author doesn't return her admiration. Soon Streep has stolen her accountant husband, played by Ed Begley Jr. As Barr lies in bed reading the rich horticultural prose of the best-selling writer – 'she entwined her limbs around him as ivy might wrap itself around some massive pillar' – Streep is making the words flesh with her husband.

Begley has an actuarial view of existence. 'Life', he informs his enormous wife, 'is made up of assets and liabilities' and there are no prizes for guessing which column she falls into. So he moves in with Streep, whose estate is smothered in pink from her mail-box to her word-processor. Barr, having exploded their matrimonial home, fires her first salvo of retribution by saddling the new couple with some unwanted liabilities: his children and her mother. The film, if it had had the snarl and bite of the television series, should have become fast and farcical. Instead, Susan Seidelman's direction is as unsurely focused as it was in her previous film, *Cookie*. Barr made the mistake of sticking to the cliché character of television comedy, she failed to appreciate that in feature films the leading players must react and develop in response to events, never more so than here.

As ever, Streep is the one who presses the pleasure button. She mastered the sincere insincerity of a best-selling romantic female author, purring 'I try to think only beautiful thoughts because then the beauty will come out in my work.' She changes from sultry temptress to serious sociologist in an all-too-recognisable piece of writerly self-deception. The real change, however, should have taken place in the casting; if Streep had played the she-devil the film could have been infinitely superior.

Working on this comedy – her first since *Heartburn* in 1986 – 'has been just a riot,' Streep said. 'I just frankly wanted to do a film that didn't cost me 75 pounds of emotional weight.' Of Rosanne Barr, with whom she actually shares only a handful of scenes, she commented, 'She's smart and sassy.'

The admiration was mutual. 'Meryl is hysterical,' Barr observed. 'She's a great comedienne. I asked her some well-chosen questions, although if I had my way, I'd be all over her 24 hours a day, asking, "What about this? What about that?"'

Streep claimed she was drawn to the script partly because of 'the issues it deals with. The issues of the woman who's dumped because she's fat and the woman who's picked up because of the way she looks. Society's preoccupation with appearances is more pronounced now than ten years ago. Look at who's in Congress, who's running the studios. I see more people having plastic surgery. It's too bad.'

She-Devil brought in approximately $15 million in the US. One would imagine this didn't leave much in the profit kitty after the two stars' fees had been recouped. Barr never really made it in the movies and eventually found her niche in Las Vegas. However the film did nothing to harm Streep's career – and she immediately made a better comedy with a better writer and a better director.

The British playwright, Alan Ayckbourn, once famously observed that 'a comedy is just a tragedy interrupted'. Few films have better underlined his axiom than *Postcards from the Edge* (1990) in which the heroine, a film star called Suzanne Vale, nearly dies after a drug overdose. She only survives after her stomach has been pumped. She is reduced to the ranks of small-time actresses, has a disastrous love affair with a double-crossing cad and an even more disastrous relationship with an overbearing mother. It sounds like a tragedy, but it's a witty and original from start to finish.

Streep must have leapt at the part although, at 40, she was on the cusp for roles as a young woman playing the dating game. However she had not yet fully demonstrated on the screen the comedic gifts that had delighted stage audiences early in her career. When Mike Nichols came calling for the third time, she had little hesitation in resuming their partnership. The wily Nichols made quite sure that America's leading film actress would take on the role by holding out a succulent cherry: she would have the chance to belt out a full-blown country-and-western number – 'I'm Checkin' Out of this Heartbreak Hotel' – at the end of the movie. Streep, after years of voice training, was delighted to have the opportunity to show how well she could sing on screen.

Carrie Fisher, who wrote *Postcards* to a large extent from life – her life – professed to be 'amazed that Meryl would play anyone remotely based on me. She told me that the emotional hook that brought her on board was just the one line "I can't feel my life".' That sounds like the ultimate disassociation from herself.

Streep was analytic as ever: 'Suzanne is very insecure and doesn't feel authentically herself. She's more like the vernacular me than any character that I've played. Her insecurities are mine, her willingness to go down the rosy path.'

When Streep did some publicity for the film she once

again laid into the studio-think that just wanted to make 'self styled blockbusters. Last summer they didn't do so well. *Days of Thunder* cost $60 million and will probably make $40 million. (In fact it grossed $80 million.) I hate to see waste. That's because I'm a mother. It appals me. Now all the studio strategists are scurrying and pointing fingers. *Thunder* had speed and boom-boom and still it didn't work. Maybe it's the voice of change. I want people back in the theatres. It's safe to go back. *Postcards* is a wonderful trip: it's smart, it's funny, and it has heart. Everybody who has a mother will respond to it.'

Perhaps Streep's true metier was the advertising business. 'Everybody who has a mother.' Doesn't that mean – er – everybody? She had correctly put her finger on a certain sea-change at the studios. It is doubtful if a male studio head would have seen the potential in *Postcards*, but Nichols cannily took the project to Dawn Steel, the newly-appointed first female president of Columbia Studios. Steel, keen to make her mark, agreed to finance it. Maybe she had a mother too.

Carrie Fisher had a famous mother, the singing film star Debbie Reynolds, and also a famous father – the crooner, Eddie Fisher, although he left the family for Elizabeth Taylor when Carrie was only two. But she became probably more internationally famous than either of them as Princess Leia Organa in George Lucas's *Star Wars* (1977) where her character was utterly memorable thanks, not least, to a hairstyle that wound her locks into the shape of two enormous Danish pastries over each ear. Lucas had at one stage considered offering the part to Streep.

The years of fame and fortune led Fisher into a lifestyle of drink and drugs. Shortly after playing April in Woody Allen's *Hannah and her Sisters* (1986), she took an overdose of prescription drugs and found herself in rehab. Fisher was known for her wit and cutting one-liners, and was prepared to talk candidly about her experience. Simon & Schuster commissioned her to write a funny, non-fiction book. At first she thought about a celebrity memoir called *Money Dearest*, but she realised this would be making fun of something she didn't want to make fun of.

Reading a Dorothy Parker story, *The Waltz*, about an alcoholic's descent into hell, inspired Fisher to turn her own story into a novel. She knew it had to be a funny one. 'I had been in an extreme situation and I made it funny to myself while going through it. That's when I needed humour, when there is nothing funny. I was in the worst place I could be and not be dead.'

Fisher sent the galleys of her book to Nichols, who was a friend. He saw the potential. But not as it stood. He knew the nature of Fisher's volatile relationship with her mother, the singer Debbie Reynolds – at the age of seventeen she had actually appeared with her on Broadway in a revival of the musical *Irene*. Nichols subtly coaxed her through successive drafts of the screenplay to centre the story around the mother-daughter relationship. In the first draft they didn't even have a scene together, but Fisher then had the inspired idea of having Suzanne being obliged by the film's insurers to lodge with her mother during the shooting of some B-picture to make sure she stayed clean.

The part of the mother had now assumed a much more significant presence in the film. Despite being painted as a self-obsessed alcoholic, Debbie Reynolds offered her own services. Nichols politely declined. He is a past master when it comes to casting and had seen Shirley MacLaine playing the crusty old crone, Ousier Boudreaux, in *Steel Magnolias*, the film set in a Southern beauty shop. He knew she was ripe for the role. She was only 15 years older than Streep but skilfully portrayed a much older woman trying to be younger in the Beverly Hills tradition, with more surgery under and over her belt than the Beast of Wildenstein.

The gags pay out right from the start. When Suzanne is informed they are going to have to pump her stomach, her response is: 'Do I have to be there?'

When in rehab her therapist gently tells her: 'I want to deal with your feelings before they deal with you.'

Her thanks are double-edged: 'Do you always talk in bumper stickers?'

A visit from her mother sets Suzanne's recovery back a couple of decades. Mom Doris is the most self-obsessed person on the planet, paying little heed to her daughter's despair and offering the hardly medical advice: 'I think you should change agents.' Looking round Suzanne's grey bedroom at the clinic she observes:

'It's so blah in here. I don't know how you can have a room all one colour.'

The competition between mother and daughter is their only way of communicating. 'I couldn't possibly compete with you,' Suzanne tells her mother. 'What if somebody won? You want me to be nearly as good as you – but not better.' This is beautifully borne out when Doris throws an unnecessarily huge welcome-home party for her daughter, encouraging her to sing for the guests. Suzanne gives a bashful rendition of the appropriately chosen 'You Don't Know Me', but finds she has just played the part of warm-up act for her old egotist of a mother. Mom takes a leg-flashing seat on the grand piano, belts out the equally appropriate 'I'm Still Here' (with new lyrics by Steven Sondheim) and upstages her daughter!

Carrie Fisher liberally cherry-picked from her own relationship with Debbie Reynolds to portray the mother figure, conceding only that 'I overdrew things.' However she did reveal that when her mother wanted her to do something, she would always say she saw it in a dream. So it is in the film: when Suzanne's manager absconds with her money, Doris saw it in a dream. When Suzanne rubbishes this the retort comes back: 'What about when I correctly dreamed you had a kidney stone?'

Streep has mused on her own anxieties and on how different she is from her mother. 'I kinda tend to agonise over things. Things cost me a lot and I just don't know why. My mother has a gift for being happy in the day. She gets up like an eight-month-old in the crib, saying

'Yippee, it's morning!' And I'm just not always feeling that way. I'm the anxious one. I don't take vacations. I don't spend money to have fun. Some days I just think 'What's it all for? What does it all mean?'

Some people might say that 'love' is the answer to such doubts. It certainly is in the film when, in the penultimate scene, Suzanne visits Doris in a hospital after she has drunkenly driven her car into a tree. With no make-up or wig, MacLaine bravely exposes her character as a scarecrow on a stick. 'That's when the mother and the daughter finally come together,' said Streep. 'There's a great deal of love between them. The mother becomes the child and the child becomes the mother.'

Mike Nichols joked that he was thinking of calling the film *Entertainment Tonight* and indeed it is more of a revue than a drama. The prolonged country-and-western song – are there any short country-and-western songs? – is very much a matter of individual taste; equally so the courtship scenes where Suzanne gives clever-clever responses to the advances of slimy Jack (Dennis Quaid) who tells her: 'I have feelings for you?'

'How many? More than two?

Or when he says 'I think I love you.'

'When will you know for sure?'

We are on steadier ground with the mother/daughter relationship. 'How would you like to have Joan Crawford for a mother – or Llana Turner?' asks Doris.

'*These* are the options?' Suzanne bites back.

Cheryl Crane, the daughter who lived through Lana

103

Turner's seven marriages and stabbed and killed her abusive boyfriend, Johnny Stompato, reported that her mother was upset by that line.

Postcards From The Edge was released in Britain during the financial downturn of the nineties. Looking at my review from then, when we were going through a recession, I said what I still feel now. 'It provided a welcome antidote':

Sunday, 27 January 1991

At times like this, a cabaret of a film is probably the best tonic, and *Postcards from the Edge* (Odeon Leicester Square, 15) certainly fizzes with fun. It even ends with a country and western song from Meryl Streep, who might well have had a career at the Grand Ole Opry.

Based on the novel by Carrie Fisher (frantic assurances are offered by all concerned that this is not a thinly disguised account of Princess Leia's relationship with her mother, Debbie Reynolds, thereby drawing attention to the possibility that it might be), *Postcards* is the story of a young actress with a drug problem who is entrusted to the care of her ageing star of a mother, who has a drink problem. It begins dramatically with an overdose, but thereafter any addiction is dealt with at the level of Carry on Coke, as Fisher attempts to get us high on the absurdity of the mother-daughter relationship.

Fortunately, her book has fallen into the hands of Mike Nichols, who shrewdly chose to cast it with actresses greater than the sum of the parts. Thus, any concern we might have had about Suzanne and her mother, Doris, is dissolved by the fact that we know we're really watching a movie about Meryl Streep and Shirley MacLaine, who wheel out a couple of all-star turns and take their bows accordingly.

Nichols hurls a few coconuts at the Hollywood community and finds some remaining shies, notably the director who informs Streep that her inflection must always go up at the end of a line in a comedy, and a cheap producer who, concerned that her performance is not up to scratch, asks her what it was they did differently in her last picture. 'Rehearse,' she replies.

Streep uses her first-rate technique to play a second-rate actress with convivial cunning, and MacLaine cloaks her domineering mother from *Terms of Endearment* hilariously with the self-deluding hubris of stardom. Men, however, do not emerge well from this film. MacLaine's father has reached a depressing dotage and her husband can't wait for his, lying ever supine before the TV in anticipation. Streep, naive for a woman of fairly mature years, succumbs to the chat-up technique of smirking Dennis Quaid, when most of the cast of *Neighbours* could have spotted him for what he was. But it leads to some good gags, the sole aim of this comedy, which seems deliberately two-dimensional – as thin as postcards, in fact.

Streep seems to have been bitten by the comedy bug, possibly rationalising that her rom-com days were finite. Why else would she agree to play the romantic lead in Albert Brooks' *Defending Your Life* (1991). It certainly wasn't a decision that she would have made after reading the script. Maybe it was one that her agent, Sam Cohn, took for her after reading the cheque from David Geffen. Or maybe, more generously, it was because Albert Brooks was a good friend of Carrie Fisher (Debbie Reynolds, it is said, always wanted Carrie to marry Albert) and Streep hoped her talented friend would beef up the material as she had in Hollywood after *Postcards*. A scriptwriter friend of mine discovered that when Carrie was brought on board to put more wit into his screenplay, her fee was a million dollars.

What was on offer in *Defending Your Life* was, if not a children's story, certainly a fairy tale. When people die they go to Judgement City where they find out they have lived many lives before. Judges look back over these lives to see if they have earned the right to go on to a special place.

If the plot seems familiar it is because it was originally written by Buddha who told his followers that they had to progress from a state of 'Anatta', where their souls passed through a succession of new bodies here on earth until they attained 'Nirvana'. Then they could go to a special place.

Brooks, himself, is an actor, a comedian, a writer and a director or, arguably, none of those things. His aim to be a second Woody Allen falls a little short of the real thing. He made his name on *The Tonight Show* with Johnny Carson where he did a self-deprecating, stand-up act that found favour with the chat show supremo. He contributed to *Saturday Night Live* in the Seventies and then turned auteur with *Real Life* (1979) – a satire on Hollywood making a reality show out of an ordinary family in Phoenix, Arizona. Brooks subsequently explained away its failure to become a hit with the dubious conceit that it was 20 years ahead of its time.

In *Defending Your Life*, Brooks plays Daniel who is cut off in his prime when his car hits a bus. In *Judgement City* he meets Julia (Streep) who died while drunk by tripping over a chaise longue, hitting her head on the side of a swimming pool and somersaulting into it. 'How many marks did the East German judge give you?' asks Daniel, one of the better lines in the film. But these are counteracted by Julia having to say to him sub-soap lines such as: 'I can't get you out of my mind' and: 'I'm going to get you.' To which he responds: 'You've already got me.' Not quite dialogue fresh from the mint.

The main attraction of *Judgement City* is that you can eat as much as you want without putting on weight – I'm not sure that Buddha would see that as entirely wholesome – and when Julia suggests they go to the Past Lives' Pavillion it is with the added incentive, 'They serve great hot dogs there.' Inside, in the individual cubicles, a woman sees film of her previous incarnation as a Sumo wrestler. Daniel was an African chief, and

Julia Prince Valiant on a horse. This spirit stayed with her in subsequent incarnations as her one-way ticket to Nirvana is purchased by having saved her children from their burning mansion and then returning to the inferno to rescue the cat. Daniel is not so lucky. It seems he will return to Earth. But if you think they're not going to get together in the end, you can't spot a cliché when it's staring you in the face.

Streep, with long blonde locks that indicate she's definitely 'worth it', looks stunning, but also a little stunned. She reacts to this stumpy, questionably funny chap with exaggerated laughter. One can see the reason for this. When they were shooting *Fierce Creatures*, Kevin Kline's agent, Rick Nicita, who also handled Al Pacino, Anthony Hopkins and Tom Cruise visited the set. He watched Kline and John Cleese rehearse a long and potentially amusing scene, with plenty of comic conflict. Afterwards John went across to him and said: 'It's not working. Why?' Rick quietly replied: 'Because you're both trying too hard.' He was right. In *Judgement City* Streep is desperately trying to compensate for the quagmire she has stepped into in this film.

But, once again, the cavalry was on the way to her rescue in the shape of true talent: director Robert Zemeckis, writer David Koepp and Goldie Hawn and Bruce Willis as co-stars – it should have been Kevin Kline but he dropped out after the studio would not pay him parity with Streep. This saviour of a film was *Death Becomes Her* (1992).

Zemeckis had already made his reputation with

Romancing the Stone (1984), *Back to the Future* (1985) and *Who Framed Roger Rabbit?* (1988), and Koepp was about to become Hollywood's most in-demand writer with *Jurassic Park* (1993) and *Mission: Impossible* (1996). Not that Hollywood is the physical or mental home for Koepp. Like Streep he chooses to live on the East Coast. I met him in his office, a comfortable apartment overlooking the scene of her early triumphs, the Lincoln Center. The reason Koepp is at the top of his profession is that he has a honed intellect topped by a very original creative mind and crafts his scenes with surgical precision. 'We always wondered how *Night of the Living Dead* would have turned out if Noel Coward had written it. One thing we never worried about was that anybody else would have our idea. We were pretty sure that we were the only walking-dead comedy.'

Death Becomes Her is a delicious piece of Grand Guignol, a satire on plastic surgery and the quest for eternal youth.

I met up with Streep after she had been on a European tour promoting the film. She observed: 'It's not just Hollywood, it's everywhere. Maybe we Americans have exported this preoccupation with youth culture but it's certainly something everybody else is gobbling up – particularly the people who are able to think about more than where their next meal is coming from. It's kinda wild.'

The film begins with a fading star, Madeline (Streep), stealing the fiancé, plastic surgeon Ernest (Bruce Willis), from her 'best friend' Helen (Goldie Hawn). Helen suffers a breakdown. Streep recalled: 'The closest character I ever played to Madeline was Frosine in *The Miser.*' Frosine is a pathological liar and a marriage broker.

The establishing shot of Helen, seven years later, is a close-up of her enormous bum. She has put on 300 lbs – the sight of Goldie (fattened by a 'flabbercast') lying on a sofa spooning a quart of ice cream into her bulbous body makes for a fairly memorable moment of comedy cinema.

Mysteriously, when Helen turns up in Los Angeles seven years later with a best-selling book, she is trim and glamorous. Madeline, by pure coincidence goes to the same New Age mystic, Lisle (Isabella Rossellini), who has done the trick for Helen. She sells Madeline an elixir that will keep her young for 10 years – after which she must disappear.

Indicating satisfied former clients, Lisle mimics one who said 'I vant to be alone' – Greta Garbo's famous line. But after Madeline has swallowed the potion, Lisle wags a finger: 'Now a warning,' and Streep echoes her: '*Now* a warning?' – doubling the laugh with her delivery.

The potion works. We see first Streep's bottom contract and then her breasts grow, firm and rounded. Meryl proudly told me: 'I take full credit for my buttocks. It was my own effect. I did that. I just flexed them. But with my breasts, they tried some balloons and all sorts of special effects, but in the end my make-up man just stood behind me and pushed them up with his hands, first one and then the other. That was the easiest way.'

Streep is superbly over the top. 'I knew from reading

the script and just walking on the set that it was all so hyperbolic, outsize and operatic in scale. So I thought this was a subtle clue for me to go a little bit wild. It's a kind of theatrical film acting you don't get to do much. In America we tend to think: 'This doesn't feel real to me'. But sometimes realism isn't what you're looking for.'

Madeline is pushed down the stairs by Ernest and ends up with her head back to front. The effect was done by putting a blue hood over her entire head and then superimposing her subsequently-filmed blue-screened face on it. Streep recalled it was the one day her mother came to visit the set and wondered why they were paying her daughter 'all that money' if nobody could see her face.

The film is a relentless assault of bad taste jokes with Sydney Pollack as the doctor who examines the reverse headed Madeline. When he finds she has no heart beat, he resorts to a swig from the alcoholic Ernest's flask. A struggling Madeline is zipped up in a body bag and taken to a crematorium where Ernest, who has been demoted from plastic surgeon to mortician, saves her from the flames.

From there the film descends even deeper into a black farce with the two Zombies, Madeline and Helen, engaged in mortal combat. Madeline shoots Helen with a shotgun and the latter staggers through the succeeding scenes with a see-through hole the size of a bowling ball where her stomach should be. Koepp's wit flows non-stop.

When Ernest worries that the neighbours will report them to the police, his wife retorts: 'Have you ever seen a neighbour in 12 years in Beverly Hills?'

Eventually Lisle's curse comes to pass and the two women end up literally in bits – still bickering, though. Streep and Hawn play off each other like a music hall act that has been tuning up its timing for years.

Streep said: 'I've had people say "You're a serious actress, how could you do that?" But for me it's a delight. You have to have food and you have to have champagne. You have to have a little bit of everything. At drama school we never did a play in a realistic setting – in three years of study, never! We weren't looking for how real people played at that point in theatrical training. I remember playing Edward II's queen in a costume that was eight feet high and eight feet wide. In another Sigourney Weaver was a lesbian storm-trooper with boots up to her thighs and an M1 rifle. And I rolled around the periphery of the audience. My main job was to yell abuse at them and, although I had certain set lines, the authors allowed me to improvise anything I liked.'

Streep at 40 was free to liberate her talents from public expectation and to flow, funny and wholly outrageous.

Streep (24) playing Constance Garnett (84), the Dostoyevsky translatrix, in *The Idiots Karamazov*. Yale Drama School, 1974.

Garnett transforms into Miss Haversham from *Great Expectations*. Yale Drama School, 1974.

With Robert De Niro. *The Deer Hunter*, 1978.

With John Cazale. *Measure for Measure*, 1976.

'Out of the two of us, I was not the psychotic, immoral, promiscuous one'.
With Woody Allen. *Manhattan*, 1979.

Henry Gummer, born 14th November 1979,
before he smashed the wine glass.

Sophie's Choice, 1982.

Meryl Streep with the author, 1983.   The author.

With director, Karel Reisz, and co-star, Jeremy Irons. *The French Lieutenant's Woman*, 1981.

Before he smashed the wine glass. With Dustin Hoffman. *Kramer vs Kramer*, 1979.

Death Becomes Her – Streep in a grand fur.

Will the nuclear plant blow up? *Silkwood*, 1983.

'He could wash her hair.' With Robert Redford,
Out of Africa, 1985.

With Clint Eastwood, *The Bridges of Madison County*, 1995.

Best Actress. Screen Actors Guild, 2009.

Streep as The Rabbi.

'I have such terrible doubts.'
Streep as Sister Aloysius.

Not playing Anna Wintour, *The Devil Wears Prada*, 2006.

On the rocks, Mamma Mia!

Still sprightly in her sixtieth year, Mamma Mia!, 2008.

16. The Gummers: Henry, Louisa, Mamie, Mary Louise, Grace and Don.

8

Was That All There Is?

And now, a confession. I fear there was a time when Streep didn't terribly care for me. There had been a bit of a misunderstanding. Ed Pressman, scion of The Pressman Toy Corporation of New York, decided to invest some of his fortune from tiddlywinks and the 'Scooby Do Haunted House Game' in the movies. He bought the rights to David Hare's play *Plenty*, about a woman, Susan Traharne, who finds the monotony of peace unsatisfactory after a romantic Second World War when she rushed about France as an undercover agent.

Pressman also hired Streep whose star was pretty high in 1984 after *Kramer vs. Kramer* and *Sophie's Choice*. The art of casting a big budget film is to get the biggest name possible at whatever price – Alexandre Salkind did this with *Superman* paying Brando $100,000 a breath to play Superman's father. Rounding up the usual suspects is then a piece of cake; the ingredients for *Plenty* were John Gielgud, Ian McKellen, Sting, Charles Dance, Sam Neil, Tracey Ullman and Hugh Laurie.

Toyland taught Ed that there *was* such a thing as free publicity so he went along to the BBC and said he would let them film a profile of Streep if they put the programme out at the time the film opened in the UK. The BBC was overjoyed.

And this is where I came in. The BBC producer, Margaret Sharp, didn't fancy doing the interviews herself and engaged me. But on our first encounter with the cast in a damp, doleful Battersea Park, Streep disappeared into her caravan before you could say 'abracadabra' – or, perhaps today, 'Abbacadabra. It seemed that Ed had forgotten to inform her that he had agreed she should be filmed for a documentary. These small omissions happen if you have a lot of things on your mind. So while the Brits gamely did their bit, talking up the project as the months of filming in Britain and France continued, the girl from Connecticut ... well ... didn't.

The relationships that develop between movie star and movie-star-interviewer range infinitely. Christopher Reeve became a tennis partner whereas William Katt stopped the interview and never spoke to me again. William Katt? Yes, he was a young actor who was deeply insulted when I suggested that looking like Robert Redford might have helped him get his part. The insolence was not as bad as it sounds; he was playing the Kid in *Butch and Sundance: The Early Days*. On *Plenty*, Charles Dance became a firm friend for the next quarter of a century. However in between takes I did ask Sting if his bank let him sign his cheques 'Sting', his real name being Gordon Sumner. He told me he had made such an arrangement with them. But when I inquired if people still called him 'Gordon' he replied: 'Only my *close* friends,' fixing me with a meaningful stare. I've always wondered if I'd greet him with a cheery 'Hi, Gordon' when next we met – but we never did.

The others were, not unnaturally, complimentary about Streep. Charles Dance, who played her diplomat husband and no mean actor himself, made the most perceptive analysis of the Streep technique of any of her co-stars: 'She leaves a lot of unanswered questions – mystery, for want of a better word. There's something else going on. She never gives you the full bag of apples. Quite a few decent ones, but you can also see that there are quite a few still juggling about at the bottom of the bag.'

John Gielgud was 80 at the time and an agreeable companion. I used to take tea with him. I asked whether Streep impressed him. She did. 'I observed her in an emotional and hysterical scene' – Gielgud recalled how her character goes berserk at a diplomatic dinner party – 'she did it about thirty times in takes and rehearsal, she never flinched or changed things except to improve them, if anything, by selectivity – giving the director something different to select from. She was completely in control of her emotions, pace, timing and her relations with other people in the scene. I was enormously impressed by that.'

Fred Schepisi, the director, did indeed do endless takes of the same scene and that – I was to learn in later years – was less about any Kubrick-like genius than taking out an insurance policy that one, or more than one, would be right.

Kubrick, on the other hand, knew just what he was doing. He engaged me to do some actor interviews on *The Shining* (1980), most notably with Jack Nicholson. Stanley filmed our interview himself one Saturday morning at Elstree Studios. When it was over Jack and I both prevailed upon him to be interviewed himself but, with his customary modesty, he declined. I think he was well aware that his mystique was best preserved in mystery.

I did however, over lunch, ask Kubrick why he did so many takes of the same scene – sometimes up to 70. And he told me. Sometimes, in an early take of a scene, he would see something wonderful from an actor which he wanted to preserve. But the rest of the scene and the people in it weren't quite right. He reasoned that if he told the actor what it was he wanted him or her to repeat they would become self-conscious and he would lose the spontaneity. So he shot – and shot, again and again, until he got the magic moment once more.

Jack Nicholson, at that same lunch, told me that if people could see him for free on TV, why pay five bucks to go to the cinema? Maybe Streep was harbouring similar thoughts on *Plenty*. So back to Battersea Park.

Ed Pressman was getting edgy; the BBC was hardly going to play this show if it was Hamlet without the prince. June Broom, the unit publicist, had become a nervous wreck at the thought of repeating the request, so the clout of Streep's formidable New York publicist, Lois Smith, was sought in order to persuade her. As luck would have it, I knew Lois. She had come out to Holland for *A Bridge Too Far* on which I was doing my usual on-set stuff, chatting to lots of stars and generals to make a documentary called *The Arnhem Report* for ITV and NBC. Lois was looking after the interests of Robert Redford and kindly took me under her wing for the next few years.

So Lois told Streep I was a good egg – well, at least, not a rotten one – and the star agreed to a short interview if she finished early on the last day of UK shooting at the National Liberal Club in Whitehall. It was a bit of a white knuckle day but Lady Luck was bountiful and the star eventually sat before the cameras in the musty library where three British Prime Ministers – Gladstone, Asquith and Lloyd George – had sat before her.

The feature unit was packing up to go to France the next day, June was lying down with her smelling salts in a nearby pub and eventually it was just the BBC lot remaining in the building. Taking advantage of the situation, I expanded our conversation to cover some of Streep's greatest hits and sheer politesse caused her to discuss them. After 70 minutes she could take it no longer and got up with the words 'I really have to go' and went.

The story has a corollary. Streep's next movie was *Out of Africa* (1985), a continent, you may recall, where her character had a farm. Universal Pictures, backer of the movie, sent Michael Baumohl and a documentary unit 10,000 miles from Burbank to the Shaba Game Reserve in Kenya to make a film of the film. But when he arrived on the set Streep informed him she would not be granting an interview. The director, the late and lovely Sydney Pollack, was taken aback. He inquired why and his leading lady said to him and Baumohl: 'Because a man called Iain Johnstone locked me in a room in London for one of these things and wouldn't release me.'

Michael (a tennis playing chum of mine) tried to persuade her that it would be hard to lock anybody up in the horizon-lapping plains of the Chaba Game Reserve, even if he were to resort to such disgraceful behaviour. But to no avail. Worse still, Robert Redford said he wouldn't give an interview either – out of solidarity. A film about the making of *Out of Africa* without Redford or Streep would be a bit like one on *Romeo and Juliet* without ... er ... Romeo or Juliet. So Universal took a bit of a financial bath on that trip.

To her credit, Streep made no mention of either of these incidents on the subsequent occasions when we met – most memorably in a televised interview at a packed National Film Theatre in London. Perhaps she had forgotten them or, more likely, me. Nothing personal in this; I could see, when we were filming in Normandy, she tended to keep herself to herself between takes. She sat beneath a spreading chestnut tree reading Frank Herbert's *Dune* which Sting had given to her (he played Fayd-Rautha Haukoman in the movie.)

118

A discreet distance away was J. Roy Helland, her towering make-up man who had accompanied her on every movie since *Sophie's Choice* in 1982. Roy started out in life as a female impersonator – Mike Nichols persuaded him to play a 'Club Hostess' in *The Birdcage* – but now had a very different role, standing sentinel over Streep to prevent any unwarranted intrusion. I reached a compromise with the star: she let Margaret's camera film her when she was doing the running about Special Operations stuff but not during her dialogue. She explained her reasoning and it seemed entirely reasonable: 'I can't get into a scene if I know I'm being watched in a different way.'

Plenty was, in essence, a message film. Susan's anger with life in a country that should be brimming with good spirits and plentiful goods after winning the war is also a parable for the decline of Britain and its loss of empire (not that many of the American audience would be particularly acquainted with the Suez crisis.) Hare had written the part specifically for his then girl friend, Kate Nelligan, who had got rave reviews in London and on Broadway. Frank Rich, reviewing it in *The New York Times*, wrote: 'As for Miss Nelligan, the Canadian-born actress known for her screen role in *The Eye of the Needle*, mere adjectives are beside the point. Only a fool would hold his breath waiting to see a better performance this season.' Nelligan had played leading parts in other movies not least as Lucy Seward in John Banham's *Dracula* (1979) opposite Laurence Olivier and Frank Langella.

119

With notices like that it seemed strange that she was dropped for the movie – or that Hare countenanced it. I talked to Streep about this. 'I felt kind of crummy taking a part that was written for Kate,' she conceded. 'She had so many years of commitment to it. I sort of side-stepped it all along the way. Then, when it became apparent that it wouldn't be made if they didn't have someone famous in it, I did it.'

David Hare, evidently, had not made Nelligan's casting a sticking point but, as it transpired, few people went to see *Plenty* and Nelligan went off to play *Eleni* (1985), the Greek mother in Nicholas Evans' popular memoir.

Plenty was not without plaudits, however. Sir John Gielgud was voted Best Supporting Actor by the Los Angeles Film Critics Association. He must have been overjoyed to get a bit of recognition, at last.

9

Later Loves

With the benefit of hindsight, it seems pre-ordained that Streep should make romantic films with the three big names of cinema, Robert Redford, Jack Nicholson and Clint Eastwood. But it almost didn't happen in the case of *Out of Africa* (1985). She had to convince a reluctant Sydney Pollack that she was the right actress to cast opposite Redford.

Pollack simply didn't think Streep was sexy enough. I know that because she said so. She has always been sensitive about being judged on her sex appeal, her reasoning being that there was no need to flaunt it like Monroe if you could act it. Streep recalled going up for a part in a Dino de Laurentis movie in 19991. 'His son kindly invited me into the presence of Dino Sr. who spoke very kindly to me. Then he turned to his son and said in Italian, "She's not pretty enough, why do you waste my time?" I understand Italian so I answered, "Non me piace molto" – I don't like that very much – and I walked out of the room. That kind of duplicity in Hollywood is so rampant. It's sick how much a woman's value is completely associated with how she looks.'

Streep had read the script and badly wanted the part of Karen Blixen so, to convince Pollack, 'I wangled a meeting at which I wore a very low-cut blouse and a push-up bra. I'm ashamed to say it but I did and it worked – that's the really sad part.' Blixen was a Danish baroness who farmed in Kenya in 1913 and, although married, fell in love with an Old Etonian, Denys Finch Hatton, a man who preferred to hunt bigger things than women.

Karen Blixen was born in Denmark in 1885 and had published short stories in her twenties. She fell in love with her second cousin, Baron Hans von Blixen-Finecke, but was spurned and married his brother, Blor (she still got the title Baroness which she rather liked). He whisked her off to Nairobi where they tried to farm coffee in the Ngong Hills, where the soil was wrong and the climate unfriendly to the beans. To make matters worse, Blor proved to be an incontinent philanderer, even giving Karen a dose of syphilis. But she fell in love with the country and the people. She recorded her life there in the elegiac book *Out of Africa*, borrowing the title from Pliny who once wrote 'Ex Africa semper aliquid novi' – 'Out of Africa, always something new.'

The story attracted filmmakers, first Orson Welles, next David Lean and David Puttnam, and then Nicholas Roeg. Roeg wanted Julie Christie to play Blixen. But none of the above came up with a script that the studios thought sufficiently commercial. It was only when Judith Thurman won the National Book Award in 1983 for her biography, *Isak Dinesen: The Life of a Storyteller*, that the love interest, which was almost totally missing from Blixen's own memoir, came to the fore in the shape of Finch Hatton.

Columbia Pictures had enjoyed a surprise success with a first script from a journalist, Karl Luedtke, *Absence of Malice* (1981) in which Luedkte wrote about what he knew about – journalism. The film brought Oscar nominations for him and Paul Newman. The director/producer was Sydney Pollack whose Mirage Enterprises delivered the studio a whopping hit the following year with *Tootsie* starring Dustin Hoffman as a woman. So it seemed logical to team Pollack with his friend, Robert Redford again and use the script writing skills of the new kid on the block, Luedtke. They needed a sweeping story for Redford who was at the pinnacle of his superstardom.

Redford wanted to play Finch Hatton as the toff he was with an upper-class English accent. But Pollack gently eased him out of the conceit, pointing out that Redford's movie star *persona* was so big that the audience would be always conscious that this was Robert Redford putting on an English accent. He was persuaded to use a soft-spoken, neutral voice and, even then, had to post-sync some phrases that had strayed into the playing fields of Eton. No such inhibition attended Streep. She recalled that Jeremy Irons had hired a Danish nanny for his children, so she persuaded him to make tapes of her which she avidly listened to before she uttered the immortal opening line 'I haad a farm in Arfrikah.'

The budget was enormous, more than $30 million.

It had to be: Pollack wanted to shoot in the original setting, the Ngong Hills in Kenya, and had a construction team work for a year to build Nairobi circa 1913. Then they had to transport lions, elephants and other animals and their trainers from the America to Africa – the movie equivalent of taking coals to Newcastle – and there was a fine fee for Pollack, an estimated $6.5 million dollars for Redford and about $2.5 million for Streep. She worked for her money spending five months on location whereas Redford, rather like his character, just flew in from time to time.

If they had stuck to the truth, with Finch Hatton as a posh bald, big game hunter, there would have been no picture. When Pollack said he needed a line to sum up what their film was about, it was Streep who shrewdly provided it – 'It's the story of a woman whose lover was more beautiful than she was.' Not only beautiful but virtually unobtainable.

Karen is faced with this conundrum: she wants to possess this romantic loner but she knows that, were she to possess him, he would no longer be the free spirit whom she loves so much. Pollack liked to make romances that are knowingly impossible and doomed to failure. With regards to Karen and Finch Hatton, he observed: 'His selfishness was his weakness and her possessiveness was her weakness. I only had one argument with Meryl and that was her reluctance to say the line "I won't allow it, Denys". I understand why she didn't want to say it but, if you don't get to the flaw, you can't finish the relationship.'

She did say it. Denys replies: 'You have no idea what effect that language has on me.'

Karen: 'In the world which you want, there would be no love at all.'

To which he replies: 'Or the best kind, where you didn't have to prove it every five minutes.'

All the greatest love stories have the protagonists facing insuperable odds and *Out of Africa* was no exception. But, of course, the lovers have their moments, most memorably one by a water hole. Luedtke was stumped for a romantic 'thing' for Denys to do while talking to Karen and turned to Judith Thurman for inspiration. 'He could wash her hair,' the author replied. Thus a Memorable Movie Moment was born. Streep recalled that she was a bit on edge while shooting the scene as there were some real, non-American trained hippopotami wandering around. She knew that if you got between them and their swimming pool they tended to eat you. Somebody had told her that more people are eaten in Africa by hippos than by lions. They are basically herbivores but make an exception in the case of humans – not many people know that.

Thankfully the hippos did not feel like lunch on this occasion, but Streep felt she had had a bit of a near-miss with a lion on the last day of shooting. Karen is obliged to defend herself from a marauding big cat with a stick but the American-trained beast refused to maraud; it just lay placidly tethered to an out-of-shot post. They were running out of time; they needed the shot, so, according to Streep, Pollack whispered to the trainer to cut the creature loose and give it a shove with Streep in the shot.

The director disputes this story. 'I love Meryl Streep so much that I would never contradict anything she said but I would have to ask any sane person if I would ever untie a lion and let it loose on my actors. I think there's a bit of 'creative memory' going on here.'

Creative memory apart, Streep knew she was in good hands. 'I had gathered from Bob that Sydney likes to work under the kind of pressure that would kill a normal man. He directed during the day and did his producing chores at night. On his days off he looked miserable. But I had faith in him. The director who tells you everything is fine is the one that you're not happy being in the hands of. Sydney worried so much that I knew he'd tie up those loose ends.'

Streep fell in love with the Ngong Hills. 'The air was sweeter than anything I ever smelt in my life and there were bird calls that I never recognised. It was paradise.' She was less in love with the notion of British colonial rule. There is a moment in the film when Karen is leaving for her native Denmark. Given her concern for the Kikuyu tribe, she is invited for a drink at the all male European club in Nairobi. Streep's attitude was 'Big Fucking Deal!'

When a director has completed a scene in the editing room, he or his editor will usually add a temporary musical track so that that they can enhance the emotional temperature. I remember on *Greystoke* (1984) Hugh Hudson used Elgar's First Symphony and so fell in love with it that he left it in. Something similar happened to Sydney Pollack. He used 'Born Free' composed by John Barry, famous for his Bond soundtracks. The music moved him, so he asked the Englishman to compose the score for the film. Barry took a look at the first scene of a train crossing the vast African veldt. 'If it had been only that,' he said later, 'I would just have been playing the scenery. But the camera settles on Streep at the back of the train and her expression has so much joy and love that I played the beauty of the countryside through her insight.' Some faces launch a thousand ships; Streep's launched one of cinema's greatest love themes.

The American reviews were generally tepid. 'Maybe the problem of the pacing is simply the nature of the beast these days with expensive period pieces. Once the difficult details are all in place, it may be too much to expect a director to resist milking every scene for more than it's worth. The character of Denys, as written by Mr Luedtke and played in a laid-back, contemporary manner by Mr Redford, is a total cipher and a charmless one at that.' (*The New York Times*). 'Redford is the fall-guy for the inescapable crass vulgarity of the whole project.' (*Village Voice*). Maybe it took a foreign eye to see that that this was not some documentary, but a romantic story in a romantic place with America's leading romantic man playing opposite its most talented actress.

In my review I wrote: 'One would have to be very hard-hearted to deny that it does work, winningly.

There may be a certain glossy magazine feel to the couple's safari courtship, but Redford remains the screen's best partner. Streep, as the dogged Dane Karen Blixen, gives an unmatchable performance that ranks alongside her Sophie. Like Laurence Olivier, she has powers of mimicry that transcend the immaculate accent and deportment of the character she is playing and seem to reach into its very soul. So convincingly does she become this woman that there is an uncanny moment, when she has spread cream on her face and stares into the mirror before bed, and it is a shock to be confronted with the famous Annie Leibowitz photograph of Meryl Streep since, by then, she has become so completely somebody else.' *The Sunday Times.*

The film took $80 million in the States and a staggering $180 million worldwide. And the Academy agreed as well. *Out of Africa* was voted Best Picture, having been nominated for eleven Oscars winning seven including those for Pollack, Barry and Luedtke. Streep was pipped to the post by Geraldine Page in *The Trip to the Bountiful.*

I wonder if Streep saw the American critical reaction to *Out of Africa* as a moment to rein back on heavy foreign accents. Her technique was unchallengeable; nobody had even seen – or, rather, heard – such an vocally chameleon film actress before. And, as Robert Redford said: 'She could play the Brooklyn Bridge – and make us believe it.' But with Isak Dinisen, was it possible that Streep sensed from the critical response that achieving a form of perfection in characterisation – not that any of us knew the dear Baroness – sacrificed a little of the emotional nexus that connected the audience to the heroine and her story?

I worked on a couple of John Cleese movies with Kevin Kline who is as close to Streep as any actor. We talked a lot about the profession and he told me that, just as on the stage you have to *ask* the audience for a laugh, so in a film you could either show the audience your performance or you could hide it. Maybe this was the moment that Streep realised she had gone too hard for the former. After that she would frequently use accents with her customary command, but always subjugate them to the character.

I watched a scene from the film recently in Meryl's company. It was the moment Blor comes to tell her that Finch Hatton has been killed in a plane crash. She is sorting some books into a packing case, looks up at him when Blor imparts the news, gives no facial register, then goes back to her packing with the words: 'Why did they send you with the news?' It is textbook screen acting. 'It's amazing how slowly paced films could be then,' she observed. 'We were allowed to be in the breath of the character. Now it's all about fast cutting.'

Streep's relationship with Jack Nicholson proved to be the reverse of the one with the Redford character in nearly every way. Was there ever a less glamorous film than *Ironweed* (1987)? The critics raved about the performances, but from the moment Joel Siegel told his viewers on ABC's *Good Morning America* that this was a 'must see film', audiences stayed away in their droves.

In fact, *Ironweed* was a badly made film, agonisingly

129

slow, bereft of drama, with a story that was as down and out as its protagonists. William Kennedy's trilogy of novels about low life in Albany, New York, had warranted his Pulitzer prize. Francis Phelan, the Nicholson wino in *Ironweed*, watches his body 'squirm into burgeoning matter, saw it change and grow with the speed of light until it was the size of an infant, saw it then yanked roughly out of the maternal cavern by his father who straightened him, slapped him, and swiftly moulded him into a bestial weed.'

Any magic realism or attempt at metaphysical transcendence became uncomfortably pedestrian in Kennedy's screenplay, his second and his last. The dead eye of the Argentinian director, Hector Babenco, did little to enhance his vision. After *The Kiss of the Spiderwoman* (1985) in which the imprisoned William Hurt invented wildly romantic movies to enable his mind and that of his cell-mate (the late Raul Julia) to occasionally escape, the producers must have thought Babenco was the one with the vision. In reality it was the writer, Manuel Puig, and the wonderful Hurt himself who made the Spiderwoman magic.

What is hard to fathom is how Keith Barish, who produced *Sophie's Choice*, managed to come up with the $27 million for this mournful film. It's not as if the actors did it for reduced fees. When Kennedy pleaded with Nicholson to come down from his $5 million the actor declined with the cryptic reply: 'I don't want a nickel more than the Bank of England will give me on my name.' The script was sent to Streep's agent and within three days the deal was done – also not, one would imagine, for peanuts.

Francis and Helen, Nicholson and Streep's characters, have been lovers for more than nine years but the romance has ceased to blossom or, as Francis delicately puts it, 'We haven't got a penny – no place to fuck.' Helen was a well-known radio singer before the wine lost her her career and, in a bar, Streep gives a fine rendition of 'He's Me Pal' in a voice that still has echoes of Helen's former glory. It would have been intensely moving if the director had not let it run for three times as long as it should.

Streep gives an all too credible performance as the decayed Helen, stumping around in the way she had seen her grandmother walk. What she catches so astutely are the changes of mood in a woman who has descended into this sad state. Warming herself by the fire at the local library, she is greeted by a woman who hasn't seen her for 20 years and wonders what happened to her. Streep uses a composed, almost well-spoken voice to lie; she has been touring Paris and Vienna. This descends into an ugly bawl as she falls out with the woman, and then a Shakespearean rant, when she is leaving the library and yells at strangers in the street. Nobody does it better. Of course, Streep and Nicholson were duly nominated for Oscars.

Streep would have to wait nearly ten more years before playing the most moving – and passionate – love story of her career. It started with a phone call from Clint Eastwood. 'Carrie Fisher had given him my

131

home phone number – I guess she hands it out to anybody,' Streep wryly commented.

Eastwood knew Streep had not enjoyed Robert James Waller's novella, *The Bridges of Madison County*. 'I had sort of half read the book and I didn't think it was something I would be interested in,' was her official comment. In fact, when her assistant had wanted to borrow her copy, she had thrown it into the waste-paper basket with the words: 'You can't read it – it's a crime to literature.'

But Eastwood assured her that the script, by Richard LaGravenese had played down the florid dialogue and said he would like her to read it. He could send it to her by courier. She agreed but, before doing so, took the precaution of renting a couple of Eastwood's movies: *Unforgiven* (1992) and *In the Line of Fire* (1993) in which he played a retired Secret Service agent – Clint's characters often had to 'come out of retirement' after he turned 60 in 1990.

Streep was impressed. 'I've never seen anybody of his age do that stuff, go out on a limb that way.' So she agreed to play Eastwood's lover in the movie. 'He made me an offer I couldn't refuse,' she joked – around $5 million, if the word on the Warner's lot is to be believed.

It was understandable that Waller's book was not to Streep's taste. *The New York Times* had noted its 'Hallmark' prose – Hallmark being the greeting cards company. *The Washington Post* had found it 'trite'. But the phenomenon of the book was remarkably similar to that of *Love Story* which Erich Segal, a Harvard professor of comparative literature, had written 25 years earlier and which became a hit film with Ryan O'Neal and Ali McGraw.

Robert Waller was a business professor at the University of Northern Iowa who had published essays on applied mathematics and management economics. He played the guitar in bars, was a keen photographer and when he was taking some pictures of the Roseman covered bridge near Winterset in Iowa the idea for the book was, in his own words, 'given to me'. He went home and wrote it in 11 days, basing the main character – a photographer who was on assignment shooting the covered bridges of Iowa for *The National Geographic Magazine* – largely on himself.

In the book Robert Kincaid knocks on the door of Francesca Johnson and asks the way to the bridge. It transpires that she is an Italian war bride. It further transpires that her husband and kids are away at the state fair – giving rise to an unexpected affair.

The rest is publishing history: The 171-page novel has been translated into 25 languages and over 12 million copies have been sold. It was on *The New York Times* Best Seller list for 3 years (number 1 for 38 weeks) and topped *Gone with the Wind* in 1995 as the best-selling hardcover fiction book of all time.

Steven Spielberg's people snapped up the rights while it was still in proof. Companies such as his Amblin Entertainment employ people known as 'golden retrievers' to sniff out projects from literary agents long before they're published. So Warners had to spill a little loose change to enable Eastwood to make the film and Amblin joined his Malpaso Productions in a share of the spoils, with Kathleen Kennedy, who produced *E.T.* (1982), co-producing with Eastwood.

Initially Eastwood did not intend to direct the movie. Spielberg expressed passing interest but had gone off at last to make Thomas Keneally's *Schindler's List* (1993). (I once stayed with Keneally in Palm Beach, Australia and his parting words when I left were: 'Can you ask Steven when he's going to make my bloody book?' He knew that I was about to work for the director who had been sitting on it for ten years; half of Steven's art is in knowing 'when'.)

Eastwood chose Keneally's fellow Australian, Bruce Beresford to direct. He had graduated from *Barry MacKenzie Holds his Own* (1974) to the Oscar-laden *Driving Miss Daisy* (1989), establishing himself as a dab hand with chamber pieces. Had Beresford stayed on the project, Streep would never have got Eastwood's call.

Quite a way into pre-production Beresford was adamant that the Italian-American Francesca should be played by an exotic European. Personally I would have thought she could have been played by a Tibetan or even an Australian providing the actress was good enough. But Beresford's desire to make Isabella Fiorella Elettra Giovanna Rossellini the love interest did not appeal to Eastwood. So he had Beresford bounced off the project and installed himself – and Streep.

Waller had written Kincaid as 52 and Eastwood was 65 but that didn't worry Warners. For so many years Eastwood had been the goose that laid the golden eggs for them. But 'the suits' were worried about Streep. It was the sex-and-looks question again. 'I was forty-five and I played a forty-five-year-old woman. But the studio thought I was too old, so Clint made a case for me, which I was glad about. I would certainly have made a case for him,' she said.

One curious factor was that, after the departure of Beresford, Eastwood was adamant that he didn't want Francesca to be Italian. But Streep put on weight, dyed her hair nut brown and spoke as an Italian woman might do, tempered by her years in the States as a war bride. Eastwood said nothing, as was his way, for most of the shoot. Eventually he felt obliged to explain to her: 'I don't say much unless I don't like it.' This certainly suited the Yale-trained actress who was playing opposite, and for, a man who got his training in the Universal talent programme and, later, *Rawhide*.

The unit set up their base in Winterset, Ohio – birthplace of John Wayne. Eastwood shot the whole film on location. And fast. Jack N. Green, his regular Director of Photography, was well-acquainted his director's impatient approach. 'Clint printed the rehearsal of the first take and then moved on. Meryl looked at the group of us and asked "Is that how it always is?" and we said: "Yes, this is how it always is. We very seldom have multiple takes and, unless you say you want to have another one, you probably won't have another one."'

135

After three days, Streep proclaimed: 'I love this way of working. I don't have to work up to anything. I can start right at the top, right at the highest note. It makes the film's emotional moments feel captured, as opposed to set up and driven into the ground.'

Eastwood, for the most part, was calm and soft spoken. But when something interrupted his concentration, he could unexpectedly explode. 'My God, where did that come from?' Streep observed of such an occasion.

'Because all day we haven't seen anything, not even a whimper. Then everybody kind of flattens into the walls and furniture.'

Eastwood had learnt to direct during the seven years he played the cowboy, 'Rowdy' Yates, in the CBS series *Rawhide*. He soon picked up the craft of getting ten minutes of finished footage by the end of the day, as opposed to two or one or less as was the practice on feature films. He was keen to innovate and, since he could ride in the middle of the cattle drive, took the camera himself on horseback to get more vivid pictures of the experience. When he started directing features, he baulked at various feature film traditions.

One night I watched Eastwood doing some scenes for *Firefox* in the Vienna underground with British actors. Instead of shouting 'Action!' he would roll the camera and start the scene with a softly spoken 'Any time you're ready, amigos.' During a break I asked him why. He said he felt a bark of 'Action!' was in danger of breaking the mood or emotion the actors had worked up or down to – they weren't sprinters running a 100 metres – and so he preferred to ease them into the filmed moment.

As far as doing just one take he felt there was a spontaneity in that moment that was hard to recapture. 'Besides, if it ain't broke, don't fix it' – although he would re-shoot, reluctantly, if anything went wrong. Streep mischievously observed: ' Even if the lights were being moved, he would say 'That was pretty good, let's move on.' Besides, he had a date on the golf course at about 4 p.m. and he made it many days.'

But Streep's respect for him was undimmed. 'It's my experience that the really great directors don't let you know *when* they're directing you, or how. You don't really know. At the end of the shot you think: 'Boy, I got to do whatever I wanted on that . You don't realise that you were subtly manipulated to do the things that *he* wanted at this point. But I felt completely free.'

The undetected art of Meryl Streep, however, is that again and again *she* contributes to the direction. She began contributing to *The Bridges of Madison County* even before she stepped on the set. The decision – against orders – to play Francesca as Italian meant that she could step into that woman. When she was growing up in New Jersey a neighbour, who was a soldier, brought home a war bride and Streep had observed and now imitated the excitable but displaced woman.

Francesca sleeps with Kincaid and pleads with him: 'Take me some place you've been, on the other side of the world.' And as he talks of Bari, where she was as a child, her passion is re-ignited, furiously. Only Jack Green was in the bedroom to shoot that scene and it is, without doubt, Streep's most convincing display of physical passion in any movie.

The map of Francesca's mind was laid out in the script. 'I had thoughts about him that I hardly knew what to do with and he read every one. Whatever I felt, whatever I wanted, he gave himself up to and, in that moment, everything I knew to be true about myself up to then was gone. I was acting like another woman. Yet I was more myself that ever before.'

In the reverse of Finch Hatton escaping from Karen Blixen, the equally maverick loner, Kincaid, implores Francesca to come away with him. When she is later in her truck in town, waiting for her husband to come from the store, she sees Kincaid for a final time. It's raining. Eastwood stands and stares at her, imploringly. There is no need for him to cry; the downpour does that for him. There is no need for Streep to speak; her face and her body tell us all we need to know about her anguish and desperation.

They should have stopped the film there, but they didn't. The bookends of old Francesca and the children finding out about the lost love just aren't necessary. The emotional power lies in the story alone – seven days that stopped her world.

Streep loved the experience of making the film – 'One of the favourite things I've done in my life.' And the way the script managed to subvert much of the cheesiness of the novella. 'It's about regret, and lost chances, and how you come to things at the wrong time,' Streep said.

10

Acquit the Dingo!

On 17th August 1980 an incident took place in Australia's Northern Territory that was to divide the nation as passionately as the Dreyfus Case had divided France 75 years previously. A young couple, Lindy and Michael Chamberlain, camped by Ayers Rock – that iconic place in the centre of the country. They came back to their tent to discover their nine-week-old baby, Azaria, had disappeared. Lindy claimed the child must have been taken away by a dingo, a wild dog. She thought she had seen it happen. A coroner's inquest agreed. The majority of the great Australian public did not.

The common opinion was that the Chamberlains were 'weird' because, first, they were Seventh Day Adventists – a seemingly anti-Ozzie cult which was against competitive sport, the true religion of most of the nation, against watching television (ditto) and had turned Sunday into Saturday; second, the couple must have gone on a lethal mission to Ayers Rock since the name Azaria means 'sacrifice in the desert' in the Bible (in fact it means 'helped by God'); third, dingoes don't attack humans (they do).

The hue and cry led to the Northern Territory Police re-opening the Chamberlain case. Azaria's bloody jumpsuit was found, an 'expert' in London looked at an ultraviolet photograph of it and pronounced there was an 'incised cut around the neck'; so Lindy had slit her child's throat. She was charged with murder and, thanks to this rather flimsy evidence, a jury found her guilty. The reluctant judge had to sentence her to hard labour for life.

It was only the discovery of Azaria's missing matinée jacket on the Rock four years later in 1986 that seemed to substantiate Lindy's story. As a result she was released and compensated. Even then many Australians were not convinced. I was working with David Frost at the time and he phoned from Australia to say he was bringing me back an 'Acquit the Dingo' T-shirt.

An enterprising British producer, Verity Lambert, who had cut her teeth on *Dr Who* at the BBC, formed her own film company, cleverly called Cinema Verity (a pun on the trendy French film movement Cinema Verité), and bought the film rights of a book on the case. *Evil Angels* was to be Verity's first feature. Verity was a friend and told me that the story had all the strength of *The Crucible*, Arthur Miller's account of the hysteria-driven trial of the Witches of Salem. I told her that I was worried that the film might never happen, since her backers were the Israeli cousins, Menahem Golan and Yoram Globus, who decorated the Cannes Film Festival each May with lurid advertisements for their forthcoming productions, few of which ever came forth.

142

But Verity was a shrewd producer. She didn't go for an Australian actress to play Lindy but had an instinct it would intrigue Meryl Streep. She was right. Gene Shalit of NBC's *Today Show* later asked Streep why she had accepted. 'I like challenges,' she told him. 'The part attracted me because of the extraordinary strength of this seemingly ordinary woman.'

So Streep set off for Australia with her husband Don, eight-year-old Harry, four-year-old Willa and Grace who was barely two. Not being a method actress, Grace's mother did not see the need to become pregnant to play Lindy Chamberlain, although the Australian was seven months gone during her trial. The pleasures of enjoying an Australian summer as opposed to the chill of a Connecticut winter were offset by the prying eyes of the Australian media. Visiting stars didn't come much bigger than Streep. She felt it was part of the territory for herself, but not for her children – one paparazzo had snapped an innocent Willa naked. Streep remonstrated with the encamped photographers, even to the extent of a physical struggle with one of them.

There were also rumours in the press of tantrums and worse on set. 'Ironically, that helped our performances,' said Sam Neill who played Michael Chamberlain. 'This was the most demanding role I've ever done, and Meryl and I felt beleaguered as the result of some tabloid fabrications, just as the Chamberlains had.'

Streep had studied all available footage of Lindy Chamberlain but was slightly reluctant to meet her in

143

person at first. She hadn't reckoned with Verity Lambert's powers of persuasion. 'I didn't want to spend too much time with her,' Streep acknowledged. 'I can't think of anything worse than being scrutinized by an actress knowing you're being studied to note your facial expressions, posture, hair-style, even the type of words you use. I feel very sorry for her but, on the other hand, I had to meet her and find out those things. They were an important part of her character since she was tried in an electronic courtroom by the media who reported and noted everything. I was frankly scared about meeting her but, when we met, she put me at my ease. She's a sharp and exact woman who says what she feels – an extraordinary, ordinary person. I wore the clothes that came out of her closet, or approximations of them.' Lindy presented her with her personal Bible for the duration of the shoot.

Streep noted: 'I didn't find her the least bit cold although she does carry everything inside. She carries her religion around like she carries her purse.' It was exactly this insight that unlocked the key to the characterization. Lindy's coldness in court underlined her guilt in the eyes of the jury. Streep understood her unnatural reaction to her baby's disappearance. 'There is a reason, she believes, that this happened. She believes that God does things for a reason. She and her husband firmly believe that someday they will be reunited with the baby.'

Streep was vehemently critical of those condemning Lindy. 'I'm fascinated by how females have to break down and cry to be vulnerable and by the fact that what she was telling was the truth but *how* she told it was annoying, unattractive and unsympathetic.'

It was not just the police who thought Lindy guilty; most of Australia did. It was bold of the director, Fred Schepisi, an Australian himself, to point up the shortcomings of his fellow countrymen and women. 'I came to realize that this was a story of public perception versus private reality,' he said. 'The public's impressions of others are generally incredibly wrong, on all sorts of levels. Here, media misinformation and wrong impressions kept refuelling each other. Eventually public perception built into something so far removed from reality that it brought about a kind of group emotional madness. It's the old pass-the-gossip routine. I tell you something, you tell it to someone else but just a little differently. By the time it reaches the tenth person, it's a totally different story.'

Schepisi added: 'In this case, a whole nation was playing pass-the-gossip. No wonder everyone was getting it wrong. One very simple example: a woman at a dinner party in Australia one evening – this is when we were shooting the film – asked me if I knew about Lindy's sister. Then she proceeded to tell me that she knew for a fact that Lindy's sister had done something weird to a baby. The implication was that this ran in the family. But Lindy doesn't even have a sister. And this woman wouldn't believe that. She told me that Lindy must have a sister because "people wouldn't make up a thing like that". These events really divided a nation. Everyone had a theory on what had really happened. It was as if nobody wanted to believe that a dingo had carried off the baby. I began to believe that there was some deep-seated need for evil in the minds of all of us. Take lawyers, for instance. They're trained to think logically. They would be in some perfectly rational discussion of legal aspects of the case, then they'd suddenly say out of the blue, "But she's guilty, of course." It was absolutely illogical.'

Streep had listened to innumerable tapes of Lindy talking so one would have thought that, once mastered, her accent would be easier than that of Sophie Zawistowski or Karen Blixen. Not so. Streep said: 'This one was the most difficult. It was part country, part Cockney, part English and it could so easily slip into any one of those types. I had to be careful to be consistent. I've gotten into trouble with accents because I take them seriously. I rarely pay a lot of attention to the dialogue before I shoot scenes. I read the script beforehand and plan the character but the actual words are secondary to the emotion I have to feel. Once I have that emotional reaction down pat, I practise the accent.'

Some Australian critics were anxious to say that no outsider can really master the Australian voice. But Lindy was born in New Zealand – and spent much of her life in Tasmania. Sam Neill, a New Zealander, himself, felt: 'Lindy's voice, with the greatest respect, is not an attractive one. It sounded at times like a fingernail on a blackboard. Meryl got it all.'

I worked with Fred Schepisi on *Fierce Creatures*. We hired him when the original director proved not quite a master of comedy. John Cleese was troubled and stayed away but I spent a week with Fred going through the previous cut of the film. His instincts on where the plot was too opaque or transparent were impressive. We talked about *A Cry in the Dark* (as the film was called in Britain and the States). Fred said the original judge had told him that he would have dismissed the case against Lindy for lack of evidence but he felt, in fairness to her, that a verdict of innocent would lay the matter more effectively to rest. His summing-up was wholly in her favour, but the jury had already made their minds up.

The film was popular in Australia and well received by the local critics. It won five Australian Film Institute Awards, one of which went to Streep for Best Actress, and she went on to get her habitual Oscar nomination. But it did little business in the States – less than $7 million on a film budgeted at many times that. It seemed the story was too insular for the insular American public, and Schepisi's films had never had wide commercial appeal – I sensed that he was a director who played to the critics rather than the gallery.

But Streep got a new and unexpected fan in Pauline Kael. Her earlier barbs about Streep's acting in *The French Lieutenant's Woman* were put to one side. Kael had watched a *60 Minutes* programme on Lindy Chamberlain and found her distant and unemotional. She went on to write: 'It is this that makes the role work so well for Meryl Streep. She's a perfectionist who works at her roles from the outside in, mastering the details of movement, voice and facial expression. She has devised a plain, inelegant walk for this woman who has no time for self-consciousness, nor thought of it, either. What gives the performance its power is that Streep can use her own aloofness and make it work in character. She has seen that Lindy's hardness saves a part of her from the quizzing and prying of journalists and lawyers – that she needs her impersonal manner to keep herself intact. From time to time, Streep suggests the strong emotions that Lindy hides in public, and we feel a bond with her – we feel joined to her privacy.'

How pleased Streep was to receive this paean from her previous scourge is unrecorded, as is her pleasure at leaving behind the ravenous Australian press pack, but she did throw them a crust as she left. She said her next movie would be *Evita* and that it would be directed by Oliver Stone, hot from his Oscars for *Platoon* (1986).

Streep has always been determined to get the roles she wants, even if somebody else has already been cast (*Sophie's Choice*) or the work was written for somebody else who took it to Broadway (*Plenty*). But even the greatest can't win every time. *Evita* was the story of the flamboyant first lady of Argentina, Eva Peron, who died of cancer, aged 33, in 1952. Tim Rice and Andrew Lloyd-Webber turned her life into a musical. One of the songs, 'It's Only Your Lover Returning', became a number one hit in the UK in 1976 when the words

148

had been changed to 'Don't Cry For Me, Argentina'. Despite the slightly hysterical response in *The Times* by Bernard Levin – 'one of the most disagreeable evenings I have ever spent in my life' – who was miffed that it wasn't an opera, the musical ran for nearly 3,000 performances in London with Elaine Paige in the title role.

When it closed in June 1983, a further incarnation as a movie was assured. Rice favoured Paige to play Evita again but nobody else appeared to. The producer, Robert Stigwood, wanted Ken Russell as director and Ken envisaged a movie with Lisa Minnelli as Evita and Barry Manilow as the narrator, Che. Mercifully this did not come to pass. Oliver Stone was then signed to direct and he wanted Michelle Pfeiffer as Evita, but others were not so sure.

Streep learnt that the part was up for grabs. She took tango lessons from Paula Abdul, polished her singing voice and recorded a tape of songs from the musical. This won over the hearts and minds of Rice, Lloyd-Webber, Stigwood and Stone.

Stone had had bad luck with his projected movie on Noriega, the colourful Panamanian who dabbled in drugs, spying for the CIA and gun running. Hollywood was unsure how popular this might be and the project was scrapped. So he was all set to shoot *Evita* in the autumn of 1987, but some accountant at the Weintraub Entertainment Group, which was going to finance the film, pointed out that the budget had escalated to nearly $40 million and that the Rice/Lloyd Webber movie musical *Jesus Christ Superstar* (1973) had grossed just $13 million in the US and the much bigger Broadway hit, *A Chorus Line* (1985) grossed a mere $5 million. So the plug was pulled.

Nobody turned the power on again until 1994 when the spotlight shone on a new Evita: Madonna. At that time the raunchy pop singer's star was higher in the firmament than that of Streep and, besides, she was ten years younger. The executives at Hollywood Pictures felt that, at 45, Streep was too old to play the life of a woman who died at 33.

Streep disagreed. In *The New York Times* of 17th March 1991 she admitted she was bitterly disappointed at losing the part. Her interviewer, Joy Horowitz, wrote: 'Ms. Streep is also a shrewd careerist who is as ambitious as any actor in Hollywood. When asked how she feels about Madonna getting the role of "Evita", a part for which Ms. Streep studied for more than a year before negotiations fell apart, she replies: "I could rip her throat out. I can sing better than she can, if that counts for anything." '

Seventeen years later, on 14th July 2008, temporary amnesia must have set in when Streep told *USA Today*: 'I would never have said such a thing. That's one of those things you can never erase from whatever it is, the Internet? Why would I say that? I was out of the running by the time they got the musical together. It's a fabulous story, though. Oh, and I don't think I can sing better than her. And I certainly can't dance better.'

A note for the psychologically inclined. Do great

actors (who have to remember their lines) suffer from a paradox of memory? They can learn their lines but their memory, for some events, perhaps, reverses especially, is as we have suggested before, *creative*. Great minds do not remember alike!

11

The Shock of the New

After her comedies at the beginning of the 1990s, Streep had starred in a series of conventional films none of which made much mark with the exception of *The Bridges of Madison County*. She needed much more challenging material. 'You wait for something that's wonderful to come and they don't come every six months,' she ruefully observed. When it came it wasn't just wonderful, it was weird and wonderful.'

It was *Adaptation*. Susan Orlean was a staff writer on *The New Yorker* who expanded one of her articles into a book, *The Orchid Thief*. It was about John Laroche – 'skinny as a stick, pale-eyed, slouch-shouldered and sharply handsome, in spite of the fact he is missing all his front teeth' – who was arrested for stealing orchids from a Florida swamp. He and his accomplices were carrying four pillow cases containing more than two hundred rare species. These Laroche planned to clone and then sell to collectors around the world. Orlean had become obsessed with the man. 'He was the oddball ultimate of those people who are enthralled by nonhuman living things and who pursue them like lovers.'

In the flesh Susan is tall woman with long red hair and slightly pronounced teeth, always laughing. 'As I was finishing the book I thought 'this will never be adapted for a film – it's very interior and non-linear.' But producers *were* interested. Fox 2000 bought the rights and, finding it virtually impossible to adapt, sold them to Jonathan Demme who brought in his *Silence of the Lambs* producer, Edward Saxon. He told Orlean he had engaged a young writer called Charlie Kaufman to do the screenplay. Kaufman was known for his unusual, not to say dangerously original vision. He had scripted *Being John Malkovich* (1999) in which somebody finds a portal into John Malkovich's brain and people go for 15 minute tours inside before being dropped back into the real world on the New Jersey Turnpike.

Some months later Saxon asked Orlean to lunch. 'It was Halloween,' she recalled. 'He said "Let's have a cocktail" – I don't usually drink at lunch – and then he said "Let's have a nice bottle of wine". And by the end of lunch I was totally drunk.

'But I said: "Can I have the script?"

'He replied: "One thing – there are some people in it who are not in the book and who you will recognise."

'"Like who?"

'"Like you".'

She read it that evening and found Susan Orlean had become a sort of drug addict who slept with her subject and appeared on a porn site. So she informed Saxon: 'You cannot make this movie. It will ruin my career.

I'm from Cleveland. You must never show this in Ohio
– my parents live there.'

But Saxon had a trump card. Orlean was won over
by the fact that Meryl Streep was going to play her in
the movie. Streep had loved the script; it represented
exactly the change she wanted now. 'Charlie Kaufman
has a fervid brain. The script is ambitious, funny and
entertaining. It just grabbed me by the throat.' She
knew that she had to hitch her wagon to a new and
different generation of film makers. The director,
Spike Jonze, best known for making videos of the
mournful Icelandic singer Bjork – was still in his twenties.
It was the career equivalent of taking a sip of Isabella
Rossellini's youth potion.

Streep appeared to agree with the *Time Magazine*
film critic Richard Corliss's assessment of Kaufman
as 'America's only provocative, intellectual screen
writer' – although I suspect David Mamet might beg
to differ.

At that time Kaufman was – as Streep's co-star in
the film, Nicholas Cage, put it – 'Not happy with who
he is in the world.' He was an extremely reclusive
man who reluctantly came out of his shell to explain
his way of working: 'Theatre is a live medium, different at every performance. Film is a dead medium. I
wanted to write something that would have a
conversation with each individual member of the
audience, which would give different experiences with
different viewings. At the time we were pitching
Orchid Thief I was finishing *Being John Malkovich*. I had

155

writer's block. I only get that when someone has paid me to write. So I put myself and my struggle into the film. After the first draft I thought "I'll never work again".'

Although fairly original for cinema, the idea of the writer being part of his work had been tried already in America. First, with Tom Wolfe's New Journalism and more outrageously with Dr Hunter S. Thompson's Gonzo Journalism, where the writer not only put himself into his work but frequently hijacked the story he was covering. When Thompson flew to Zaire for *Rolling Stone*, to cover the Rumble in the Jungle between Muhammad Ali and George Foreman, he decided not to go to the fight and spent the time floating in his hotel swimming pool as he couldn't bear to watch his fellow Kentuckian, Ali, being beaten – he wasn't.

Streep was eager to be involved when someone was bold enough to try and put some post-modern on the screen. The public – and producers – often misread her as the Homecoming/Ice Queen, but underneath the serene exterior is an artistic rebel, honed by her years at Yale, somebody as eager to rewrite the rules of cinema as Kaufman was.

Kaufman even found time to attack the guru of screenwriting, Robert McKee, who laid down a template for scripts which, he insisted, must have a classic story design with reductive emotional arcs. I have to own up to the fact that Cleese and I attended a McKee weekend seminar and it came in useful when a young Universal executive found a flaw in the 'third act' of our screenplay, all studio executives having been brainwashed by the swami. Kaufman even puts McKee (played by Brian Cox) into his own film and has him deconstruct the whole narrative from within – 'this is your basic education plot, criss-crossed with a dis-illusionment plot'. He rebelled even more against McKeeism by leaving out the third act completely. The film just fizzles out at the end of the second.

The approach appealed to the actors. Nicholas Cage, who played Kaufman in the film, observed: 'Like poetry, you don't have to know exactly what's happening. You just feel something and connect with it.' Cage not only played Charlie but also his brother, Donald, a McKee disciple who makes a million out of writing a slashing, serial-killer movie while Charlie suffers to make something artistic which will not make vast profits. Kaufman even dedicated the film to Donald although he does not, in fact, exist.

Streep said of *Adaptation*: 'It was funny and entertain-ing but also profoundly sad and ambiguous at the end. The script tries to operate on a lot of different levels all at once. You're not left with a tidy package. It's the sort of film I like.'

Streep added with a certain modesty: 'I couldn't find out why they wanted me in this part. I figured they should get somebody younger and prettier.'

The plot is as impenetrable as Florida's Fakahatchee swamp where Susan and Charlie wind up chasing down John Laroche (played by Chris Cooper). Charlie's story leaps around like a grasshopper, at one moment settling on the impossibility of him telling the story, then theorizing on Darwin, then on his masturbatory moments but finds lucid intervals when he actually manages to tell the tale. Charlie wants 'the truth' in order to have a real experience on which to base his screenplay. He would also quite like to have Susan but she has formed an unrequited passion for the toothless orchid swindler, her passion inflamed by his passion for the flower.

Streep didn't try to impersonate Susan Orlean. Instead she created the character from the fine-tuned prose of her book which she reads in a measured manner. At the start of the film everything about her is careful, even wary. But just as Laroche is defined by his passion, she becomes defined by hers and she changes into a teenager in love, improvising moments from her youth as she cradles her bedside hotel phone in excitement, getting high on her potential lover's ring-tone alone. Streep, herself, deeply into the part, devised the romantic moment when Susan teaches Laroche to harmonize a note with her over the telephone.

'On our first day on this movie, Nick and I filmed this dream seduction scene. I walked in, shook hands and climbed on top of him,' she laughed. 'There was none of this sensitive, bonding stuff. In fact my biggest difficulty was dealing with Nick because he makes me laugh. He's so funny. I couldn't help it. He'd send me into laughing spasms. There wasn't that much laughing when Chris got on the set. He's a little more professional than Nick and me.'

Again Streep was nominated for an Oscar, as were Nicholas Cage and Charlie Kaufman and even his brother Donald. The Academy every nominated a non-existent person before? But the only winner was Chris Cooper as the malodorous hero of the original novel.

Even with the publicity of the award season – Streep won a Golden Globe for Best Supporting Actress and the film was high on the list of every Critic's Circle, reflecting the nearly unanimous praise given to it in most reviews – *Adaptation* was never going to be a blockbuster. It knew its audience and its audience knew it.

You wait decades for a meaty, post-modernist script to come along – and then two arrive in the same year! That's what happened to Streep in 2001.

The Hours (2002) attracted a much wider audience and higher box-office gross than anybody involved might have dared hope. It dealt with the subject of the novelist, Virginia Woolf, and that would usually guarantee multiplex audiences scrambling for the exits. But Michael Cunningham's sensitive, magical, interior novel, *The Hours,* inspired by Woolf's *Mrs Dalloway* (which she originally had been going to call *The Hours*), won the Pulitzer Prize for Fiction in 1999. It shot past Stephen King to the top of the Amazon best-seller list.

Cunningham claims that as a high school student he had never heard of Virginia Woolf until a girl in his class taunted him about his lack of literary knowledge.

159

He must have heard of the Burton/Taylor film *Who's Afraid of Virginia Woolf?* (1966), but that wasn't about Virginia Woolf at all. The writer, Edward Albee, merely called it that because he had seen the phrase scrawled on the wall of a bar and it stuck in his mind, being the same rhythm as 'who's afraid of the big bad wolf'. He used it for his play which, he said, concerned 'who's afraid of living life without false illusions.'

Stung by his fellow student, Cunningham made for the school library where the only Woolf book was *Mrs Dalloway*. It blew him away. When his own novel was published, more than 30 years later, he recalled: 'Something about what she was doing in trying to find the profoundity in the most outwardly ordinary experience registered with me and has stayed with me ever since.' Charlie Kaufman would have got on well with Virginia; like him, she eschewed the traditional, linear story and climbed into the minds of her characters, eager to explore the way that time is experienced, both as a sequence of disparate moments and as the flow of years and of centuries.

Mrs Dalloway, published in 1925, takes place in the course of a single day with Clarissa Dalloway at its centre. But time wanders backwards to her pre-war days when, amongst other things, she harboured longings for another woman. Woolf, although married and a mother, had a long, lesbian affair with Vita Sackville-West.

In *The Hours* Cunningham interlocked the lives of three women living at different times in different places:

Virginia Woolf (played by Nicole Kidman) is semi-suicidal in the London suburb of Richmond upon Thames; Laura Brown (Julianne Moore), a depressed housewife in 1950s Los Angeles is reading *Mrs Dalloway*; and Clarissa Vaughan (Streep), a lesbian publisher living in present-day Greenwich Village is preparing a party for a gay male friend who is going through the last doomed stage of AIDS. In fact in real life Virginia Woolf drowned herself in 1941 in Sussex.

The Hours seemed a pretty uncommercial project but Scott Rudin, a Hollywood wunderkind who was President of Production at 20th Century Fox at the age of 27, felt passionately about it, as it was written by a fellow gay man and addresses the subject of same sex love. Rudin said: 'If you're going to spend two or three years of your life working on something, you've got to be making the kind of movie that discusses and influences the culture and is engaged in the world you're living in.'

Celebrated as Streep was at that time she was not, in Hollywood patois, 'bankable'. But Nicole Kidman was. Not only had she got *Batman Forever* (1995), *Eyes Wide Shut* (1999) and *Moulin Rouge* (2001) under her belt but she was in the papers every day thanks to her marriage to Tom Cruise which he mysteriously terminated in 2001. She was flattered to establish her gravitas by playing Virginia Woolf and it had the added bonus that she would be able to wear a false nose. Actors love false noses. Laurence Olivier donned one at every opportunity. The poor prosthetics man on *The*

Hours found himself ineligible for a Best Makeup Oscar because the nose was digitally touched up in post-production.

Stephen Daldry, a British stage director who had moved into films with *Billy Elliott* (2002), was signed to direct.

Streep is candid about her involvement in the project. 'Initially, I turned it down. I have varying degrees of confidence and self-loathing. Usually I have a lot of doubt. I always say to my husband, "I've never felt like this before," and he goes, "No, you do this every time. You dismantle yourself before you begin. This is your process." I always feel like I can't do it, that I can't go through with a movie. But then I do go through with it after all. It was very delicate and very underwritten. A lot of it depended on whether or not it could play musically.'

What made Streep decide was talking to the director. 'He had a vision about it. So, I turned around and said yes.'

The Hours is a sombre film which begins and ends with a suicide. There is the odd moment of delightfully unintentional humour – at one stage Woolf tells her husband that if she were forced to choose between Richmond or death she would choose death. But, unlike *Adaptation* there is something a little too tidy about *The Hours*, not entirely different from being shown the pattern in a tapestry or symphony. Indeed if you're not sure what highs and lows you *should* be feeling during the film, Philip Glass's mathematical-sounding score keeps you on track. Laura Brown spends nearly a whole day making the perfect birthday cake for her hard-working husband. Virginia Woolf dutifully stays with her husband, Leonard, (or rather fails to escape on a train to London without him stopping her on the platform) rather than pursuing femme fatales. Even in the 21st century, Clarissa Vaughan constructs her whole day around the party she is throwing in honour of Richard – her one-time lover, and tells him it doesn't matter if he would rather not show up. She'll throw the party just in case he deigns to make it.

Clarissa is something of an enigma. She has an unexplained back-story, namely that she had a heterosexual love affair with Richard, a child by artificial insemination and now prefers kissing women, which Streep does rather well. But what caused this sexual sea-change? We are not really told.

Streep's scenes were filmed first, then Julianne Moore's and finally Nicole Kidman's. The lives of the three women are interwoven but they never actually meet until an elderly Laura encounters Clarissa towards the end of the film. Rudin feared that Julianne couldn't successfully be aged and so they got Betsy Blair to play her as an older woman for her scenes with Streep. Daldry didn't think that worked so Streep was recalled to do them again with a successfully wrinkled Moore.

Streep seemed utterly in her element, almost as if the frosty lesbian mother she played in Woody Allen's *Manhattan* back in 1979 had grown up into a contented, liberated fairy godmother to anyone who might need her.

The film was made for the relatively modest sum of $22m but grossed more than $40 million at the North American box-office. It was showered with respectful reviews and prizes; the studio put Nicole Kidman up for Best Actress – although she had the smallest part (30 minutes to Moore's 33 and Streep's 42). The Academy lifted her out of her despair after her marriage to Tom Cruise ended. She won the statuette. 'Meryl Streep just raised the bar,' she said. 'I mean, she is the great one and she really set the standard for all the rest of us.'

Streep was going to the ball anyway, having been nominated as Best Supporting Actress for *Adaptation*. Somewhat cruelly she was up against her *Hours* co-star, Julianne Moore, but neither of them won. It went to Catherine Zeta-Jones for *Chicago*. It could have been worse: it might have gone to Queen Latifah.

For Streep this bi-annual fixture was becoming a day out for the family. 'I have four kids and I've taken three of them to the ceremony. Since she went, the 11-year-old is, like, 'When do the nominations come out?' I go, `Shut up, already.' She just wants to go and see stars, and I say, 'I'm a star.' But she's not buying that.'

12

Angels in Disguise

No director has had a greater influence on Streep than Mike Nichols. They collaborated successfully in *Silkwood*, *Heartburn* and *Postcards from the Edge*. Nichols had his finger on the pulse of the American media and, after directing the universally derided 'comedy' *What Planet Are You From?* (2000), sensed that there was no immediate prospect of getting a quality movie financed by the Hollywood studios. But, on cable television, Home Box Office was providing some of the best drama with *The Sopranos*, *The Wire* – about the inner city turmoil of Baltimore – and, on the lighter side, *Sex and the City*. No studio would touch Tony Kushner's challenging seven-hour play *Angels in America*, but HBO would.

Nichols was able to persuade Streep to switch to the small screen with the lure of no fewer than four different parts. They hadn't worked together for twelve years and a serious rift between them at the end of 1990 almost meant that, at one stage, it was unlikely that they would ever work together again. The rift was caused by a book. Kazuo Ishiguro, born in Nagasaki but educated in England, had written a Booker prize-winning novel, *The Remains of the Day* about a repressed romance between the housekeeper and the butler in a stately home in pre-Second World War England. Harold Pinter optioned the rights while it was still in proof. Who better to play the pair than the stars of *The French Lieutenant's Woman* – Streep and Jeremy Irons – and who better to direct than her favourite director, Mike Nichols?

Pinter wrote the screenplay and Nichols reunited Streep and Irons for a read through. All were enthusiastic but ... it didn't happen. Was it that Columbia wouldn't meet the $23 million budget for a sort of art house film or was it that Nichols didn't feel that Streep and Irons were right for the parts? I don't know and Streep doesn't know. The project was subsequently handed over to Ismail Merchant and James Ivory, with Emma Thompson and Anthony Hopkins now playing the leads and, amazingly, Mike Nichols staying on as producer. Streep's anger can hardly have lessened when Nichols was nominated for an Oscar, and so was Emma Thompson.

Nichols failed to tell Streep that she hadn't got the part. Neither did her agent, Sam Cohn, who knew about it because he was Nichols' agent. Can it be that both men were afraid to? 'Mike is someone I share an enormous part of my history with,' Streep said of the incident.' He has a big part of my heart.'

But, as with a Roman emperor, Streep chose to take revenge on the messenger who brought the bad news – or, in this case, didn't – Sam Cohn. In an unheard of gesture, she fired him.

'I left because of something that Mike did that I thought Sam should have protected me from,' she said. 'Mike knows what he did but unfortunately Sam wore the scar.' She didn't just leave Cohn, she left New York to refresh her career in Los Angeles and her family went with her to a large house in Brentwood. The Creative Artists Agency, under Michael Ovitz, ruled the town and they made their new client very welcome.

If one ever wonders what goes on beneath the outwardly cheerful, composed exterior of Meryl Streep, that gesture certainly speaks volumes in terms of her ambition, ruthlessness, priorities and passion.

Her flight to Los Angeles did not last many years. It is a town devoted to deals and its culture – or lack of it – was hardly going to be comparable to that found in New York. So, after not many years, she relocated back on the East Coast, citing the need for all the children to be in the same area for school.

This brings us back to *Angels in America*. Streep knew the play – it had started life in 1990 as *Millennium Approaches*, a workshop piece developed by the playwright, Tony Kushner, with the Center Theatre Group in Los Angeles, with a second half, *Perestrokia* added two years later. Both works, which ran three and a half hours each, played back to back on Broadway; both were awarded Tonys for Best Play plus a Pulitzer Prize. They operated on two levels: as serious, heartbreaking dramas about the AIDS epidemic and as a witty, evocation of gay life in contemporary America. When the plays were written AIDS looked like becoming an incurable plague and Reagan was in the White House, an easy target for liberals. Kushner widened his canvass to include all those oppressed – racially, religiously, politically and socially.

The story centres on two men with AIDS. One is a 30-year-old named Prior, who is abandoned by his boyfriend, Louis, after revealing his illness. The other is Roy Cohn, the real-life, power-hungry lawyer who refuses to come out of the closet. Prior receives visits from his ancestors' ghosts and a beautiful angel, who declares him a prophet. Meanwhile, Ethel Rosenberg haunts Cohn; he had pressed for her execution, although it was her husband, Julius, who spied for the Russians. Ethel was innocent.

Prior and Roy never meet, but the lives of the people they know intersect. The connections are complicated, sometimes unexpected. Louis beds Joe, a married Mormon with ties to Roy; Joe's dowdy Mormon mother Hannah befriends Prior; and Prior's best friend Belize, a flamboyant black, gay nurse, tends to the racist Roy. There is a moving climax when those who survive meet at the Bethesda fountain in New York's Central Park – the waters of the original, in Jerusalem, were said to have the power to cleanse the soul.

'Initially, I worried that there isn't enough anger in Angels,' Kushner recalled. 'I was concerned because being polite in political activism is not a very effective tool. You can't persuade people who are basically out to destroy you that they shouldn't do that by being nice to them.'

But it didn't worry the critics. John M. Clum, Professor of English at Duke University, called the work 'a turning point in the history of gay drama, the history of American drama and of American literary culture. It is structured like a Shakespearean romance. A seemingly stable world atomizes to be reconstructed and redeemed. Relationships are quickly brought to a crisis point. Destiny or coincidence causes unlikely collisions. Characters thought dead miraculously reappear. The real and the dream merge. Seemingly disparate actions are analogous. Comedy and tragedy alternate and, at times, coalesce.'

The New York Times, too, had had high praise for the innovative writer: 'Some playwrights want to change the world. Some want to revolutionize theater. Tony Kushner is that rarity of rarities: a writer who has the promise to do both.'

The rift between Nichols and Streep was short-lived. She said of her spat with him: 'I was very upset to be upset. I have too much need for a forgiveness in my life.' And so she forgave him.

Now he lured her back into the television version of *Angels* with the inducement of the four parts and an assured vast audience. It gave her the chance, after a friendship of 27 years, to act with Al Pacino. He had been John Cazale's closest friend and mentor. Streep told him: 'I remember in the old *Godfather* days walking around with you downtown. It was horrible. People would scream at you. I determined I was never going to get famous.' Now Pacino was regarded as one of the country's foremost screen actors with seven Oscar nominations and a win for *Scent of a Woman* (1993) under his belt. Like Streep, he had mixed a combination of commercial cinema and less widely popular projects like *Looking for Richard* (1996) – his quest for an interpretation of *Richard III* which he directed.

Streep was clearly keen to do the piece but needed reassurance from Nichols as to why he was confident it would work on television. 'I thought the play was amazing and, in its time and place, it just sort of radiated heat,' she told him. 'But it was a theatrical experience I thought could never be achieved in any other medium. It's such an act of bravery and recklessness, a sort of young man's challenge. (Nichols was 73 at the time they made it.) Not that you're not young in your mind and in your outlook but I'm in awe of that starting place that says 'Yes, I think I can do that.'

The director said he had a purely instinctive response when he read it. 'I could never understand all six and a half hours in time to shoot it. I'm not that kind of scholar.'

When the play's producer had told Kushner that he was taking the project to Mike Nichols to see if he could make a film of it, the writer was extremely sceptical. AIDS was no longer the headline news that it was when he wrote it. Then it had been killing more than 50,000 Americans every year; now the total was well below 20,000. But in the interim a new and almost as frightening a disease had hit America with 2,762 of them dying in its first wave: terrorism. The World Trade

Center fell on 11th September 2001. Nichols could see that the country which had embraced him, a Jewish German refugee, was in danger of reneging on the promise written by the poet Emma Lazarus and inscribed on the Statue of Liberty.

'Give me your tired, your poor, your huddled masses yearning to breathe free.'

Kushner liked the fact that Nichols didn't want to shoot it as a period piece. He said: 'The world had changed enormously since the play was written – and thank God. But I was scared about that in terms of the film. I thought, "Isn't just going to be very old hat?" But the way Mike made it, it didn't insist that you go back into the period by shoving it at you – "this was back then, when things were like this". It simply used the basic tools of drama – empathy and compassion – and said "this kind of suffering was the result of this kind of oppression". After all, you can immediately sympathize with what Nora is going through in *The Doll's House.'*

Angels brought Streep face to face with Emma Thompson, the actress whom Nichols had engaged in place of her to play the housekeeper in *The Remains of the Day.* The two women got on splendidly. Since they were both playing flying angels – Emma was also Nurse Emily and a Homeless Woman – they were occasionally conjoined for blue screen sequences. A blue screen sequence is filmed against a blue coloured screen which can then be replaced with all kinds of wonderful backgrounds. 'Our breastbones were literally tied together,' Emma recalled, 'there were like six inches between us. And our glasses knocked as we put them on to look at the monitor. We were shrieking with laughter.' They are strikingly similar women, both immensely well educated actresses; Thompson went to Cambridge University and is the only woman so far to have won Oscars for Best Actress – *Howard's End* (1992) – and for Best Adapted Screenplay – *Sense and Sensibility* (1995).

I first clapped eyes on Emma at the Edinburgh Festival in a Cambridge Footlights Revue along with Hugh Laurie who had been her boyfriend. They were brilliant and I invited them and the rest of the cast to adapt the show for a late-night BBC 2 programme I had devised in 1979 entitled *Friday Night ... Saturday Morning.* I suppose I must have been the first person to put her on national television – and Hugh, too, come to that. Emma had just ceased being a teenager but was nevertheless a determined young woman. When I suggested, in rehearsal, she remove a rather ugly long stole to show her feminine shoulders when she sang her melancholy love song, she refused, point blank. 'Why?' I asked. 'Because I've got a big bum,' came the blunt explanation. There was, as the late Eric Morecambe was wont to say, no answer that.

But I was happy to read in the promotional coverage of her roles in *Angels* when she admitted she had never seen the play, 'I didn't have that dreadful responsibility towards an iconic role. I just fretted about the usual things like – does my bum look big in this?' After nearly a quarter of a century, some things don't change. Thompson and Streep, both fine featured women but not quite, say, conventionally gorgeous, have a magical quality few other actresses possess: if they choose, they can 'play' beautiful.

One of Streep's parts was as an 80-year-old rabbi who counsels Louis. She drew inspiration from her family. 'The rabbi embodied my father. I didn't realize this until I saw it. My father was there and I didn't even know I was doing it. I wasn't really thinking about much. I did go to Williamsburg and had some kreplach, you know, 'to prepare' (Williamsburg in Brooklyn has a large community of Hassidic Jews and kreplach, especially in chicken noodle soup, is a favoured Kosher dish.) Streep was so convincing that, after she had spent a morning dressed as a rabbi, in make-up and using the 'scrabbly' voice she had worked on, ad-libbing with her two fellow rabbis, played by Kushner and the celebrated illustrator Maurice Sendak, who turned to Kushner and said: 'When is Meryl Streep going to turn up? I thought she would be on set today.'

Tony then revealed to him that the other rabbi *had*, in fact, been Streep.

Sendak yelled: 'I don't believe it! I don't believe it!'

Streep confessed to being tickled by this. 'I felt better, too, because actually he had been kind of distant from me all morning – nice, but reserved – and my feelings had been a teeny bit hurt.'

Streep at Yale Drama School and Pacino at the Actors' Studio under Lee Strasberg had very different training.

Yale taught the Stanislavski method of getting into the character and finding emotions from the character's memories whereas Strasberg forced actors to delve into their *own* memories, sometimes making them confront their 'pain'.

Yet the two stars had a common approach to their parts. It was, quite simply, that they would make the best possible case for their characters. Streep did this for Hannah, the Mormon mother who is lost in New York. 'I always loved that idea – defending a character from judgements that are made right off the bat. You make a decision about this character that maybe she's someone who's ignorable. In an airport you see millions of these ladies in mauve coats with white hair and features that sort of blend into their clothing. They're like walking errata. They're lost, you can't find them and you wouldn't possibly be interested in them. But Tony was interested in Hannah and the possibility of her, the size of her journey.'

Roy Cohn, as written and in life, was a reprehensible man, a right-wing bigot, an utterly immoral lawyer who abused his power and a gay-hating gay. But Pacino found some sympathy within. 'I had seen Ron Liebermann and F. Murray Abraham play him on Broadway. There's something about seeing someone you're going to play that's almost a model, it's almost like 'Somebody did it, so therefore it can be done.' It sanctions it for you. I didn't set out to make him sympathetic. I think it was innate in the characterization that Tony made. He's already done the work and so it's up to you to sort of find it in yourself and follow his lead.'

Emma Thompson remarked that Cohn reminded her of Satan in Milton's *Paradise Lost.* 'You're so fascinated by Satan – he's the best character.'

Streep agreed with that analysis. She pointed: 'We love characters like Roy Cohn, Richard III, Hannibal Lecter. We love the monsters because you're entertained by them and you imagine that they're not like you – but that's the thing that really pulls you in. There is a connection. Revenge. It's a great thing to get, isn't it? And Roy can do it. He can pick up a phone and get revenge on anyone. And you wish you could do that.'

Pacino, guardedly, acknowledged that he used aspects of himself. 'Certain things, you relate to. I don't do this consciously, mind you. All I do is keep looking at the role and think, "It's a blank canvas. I don't know what the hell to do!"'

'Why did they hire me?' Streep interrupted, in an interview they did together with *Entertainment Weekly.* '"I gotta get out of this." That's what I always think.'

Pacino agreed: 'Yeah, and then I finally realize, "But I can't just go quit, so I have to do something." I'm not kidding. This happens most of the time. I did look at Roy Cohn films, knowing it wasn't going to help me that much. But it still gave me something to focus on. For me, I love the whole idea of sitting with something for a period of time absorbing it. Just being alone with a role, living with it, thinking about it. But when it comes to a guy like Roy Cohn I don't like to think I have anything in common with him.'

In an American Film Institute Tribute to Pacino, Streep said how exciting it was to watch his attention to small details. 'He makes acting count, like it's something important.'

When *Angels* was completed, Nichols went with his wife, the television presenter Diane Sawyer, to the premiere.

'She said "You keep talking about what it's about, but only I know what it's about."

'I said "Okay, if you're so smart, what's it about?" and she said "Being Jewish".'

The television transmission of *Angels in America* on 7th and 8th December 2003 was the most watched made-for-cable movie of the year and was received with almost universal acclaim. Frank Rich in *The New York Times* caught the mood: 'There is much, much more to *Angels* than politics, which is why it is so gripping. Were it a didactic ideological piece, it would be deadly. But Mr Kushner's story is built on characters, gay and straight alike, who fight timeless battles over love and betrayal even as they struggle with the meaning of faith, family and America itself at an apocalyptic moment in the life of their nation. In the nearly dozen years since the play's premiere, its captivating interweaving of fevered dreams with domestic drama, of humor with death, has become a calling card for adventurous TV, including HBO's *Six Feet Under* and

Carnivàle as well as *The Sopranos*. And if anything, Mr Kushner's writing has gained in pathos with age. What he has to say about coping with unfathomable loss and the terror inflicted by covert, death-dealing cells at the end of the last millennium speaks to us more urgently than ever in the new one ushered in by 9/11'.

Streep had forgiven Nichols without reservation. After the shoot, she said: 'Mike is much more relaxed and confident and just as delicious and inventive as ever he was. He lacerates you with *bons mots*, he levels you with his wit and makes you feel omnipotent with the freedom he gives you. He's incapable of earnestness and of saying anything that isn't funny, deeply funny – even, and especially, criticism for which he saves his best material. When you're laughing, it all goes in easier. And I don't know any other director on earth who would've immediately and without reservation asked me to do these characters and then left it entirely up to me how they'd look, act and talk. He trusted me and it's that confidence in his actors that makes people want to work with him again and again and again.'

Again, Streep was revelling in assuming some of the work a director does.

Angels swept the 2004 Golden Globe Awards with Streep and Pacino winning Best Actor and Best Actress. When it came to the Emmys – a very recherché name, emmy being the feminization of 'immy,' the slang term for the image orthocon tube used in television cameras – *Angels* won 11 awards out of 21 nominations, breaking the record previously held by *Roots*. Nichols, Kushner and Pacino all picked up theirs. *Angels* also won Best Mini-series.

The list of nominees for Outstanding Lead Actress in a Mini-series or Movie was widely agreed to be the strongest in living memory: Glenn Close for *The Lion in Winter*, Helen Mirren for *Prime Suspect*, Judy Davis for *The Reagans* and both Streep and Emma Thompson for *Angels in America*. Between them they had 22 Oscar nominations, four outright wins and one more to come when Dame Helen became 'The Queen'. But the name that Treat Williams pulled out of the envelope on the night of 25th January 2004 was Meryl Streep.

She was on wickedly funny form in her acceptance speech. 'You know, there are some days when I, myself, think I'm overrated. But not today. Glenn (Close) is my friend, so I know she'll forgive me. Helen Mirren is an acting god, and nobody has put a better performance on film than Judy Davis in *The Judy Garland Story*. The only one in the group who will hold a grudge for the rest of her life is Emma Thompson. But who cares?'

The joke went down very well and doubtless kept Streep warm for the remains of the day.

13

Family Matters

27th May 2004 was proclaimed 'Meryl Streep Day' by the Borough President of Manhattan, Virginia Fields. It was at a lunch for 800 guests at the Marriott Marquis Hotel on Broadway to honour Streep with a Career Achievement Award.

'You would have thought they could have suspended alternate side of the street parking on my behalf,' she joked afterwards. 'But no.' In fact she had arrived by cab but when she went to hail one after the ceremony she was cut off by a woman claiming she'd been there first. 'But it's Meryl Streep Day!', the star complained and woman relented, shared the ride and paid the fare. Her trophy cupboard was further crammed when she flew to Moscow the following week to be given the Stanislavsky Prize.

As well as the family home in Connecticut, Streep has always kept a foothold in Manhattan, regarding herself as a native New Yorker. She still has a preference for Greenwich Village where her husband, Don, had to build an extra room in his studio so she would have somewhere to sleep before their romance began. Now, with four children, they need something bigger. The 6,800 square foot town house was five stories high with seven bedrooms, a garden and roof terrace, and was sold to the pharmaceutical heiress, Elizabeth Ross Johnson. Rumours say it has recently come to the market again for $16.8 million.

It is self-evident that Streep has accumulated a substantial fortune from her work. It would be pointless to estimate exactly how much, but the back-end deals on films such as *The Devil Wears Prada* and *Mamma Mia!* could well run into tens of millions of dollars. She has confessed that she is something of a workaholic, reluctant to take holidays or spend extravagantly.

She has, however, made commendable use of her fortune and her time in supporting charities. Closest to her home in Connecticut is that of a former neighbour, the late Paul Newman. In 1988, he founded 'The Hole in the Wall Gang' which takes 800 seriously ill children every year and teaches them creative ways of self-expression through acting, dancing and singing. Streep has immersed herself in this and even appeared in a stage play with them, *The World of Nick Adams*, in which she was joined by Julia Roberts.

She is also Honorary Chairwoman of 'The Connecticut Farmland Trust' which is devoted to protecting remaining farmland for agricultural use, has helped to raise funds for 'The Hudson Valley Preservation Coalition' – to preserve the river and its environment – and she initiated the 'Stop the Plant' poster campaign, anxious to prevent the establishment of new nuclear facilities.

She joined Jane Fonda and Susan Sarandon in 'Taking Action for the Human Rights of Women', lobbying George W. Bush for the civil and social rights of American girls and women. Streep has used her fame to front films for 'The Grace Children's Foundation' to provide funds and medical care for China's orphans, 'What Should I tell my Children about Drinking?' for the National Council on Alcoholism and Drug dependence and *Stolen Childhoods*, a documentary for Amnesty International to try and stop impoverished children being exploited and find them an education.

Streep also gives, often anonymously, to Elton John's 'AIDS Foundation', 'The American Paralysis Association' and 'The Children's Health Environment Coalition'.

Don Gummer has also moved on from the days when he could create his sculptures in a small studio. For a while he favoured architecturally influenced installations but now he creates large-scale abstract sculptures like the stainless steel and stained glass 'Southern Circle', standing 25 feet tall and weighing 20,000 lbs, which was commissioned by the city of Indianapolis and dedicated in October 2004.

All their children seem to be following, one way or another, in their mother's foot-steps. Henry, who will be 30 in 2009, is an actor, film-maker and co-founder of a rock group called 'Bravo Silva'. Mary Willa, better known as Mamie Gummer, studied Communications and Theatre at Northwestern University. She graduated in 2005 and the same year appeared off-Broadway in Noah Haidle's *Mr Marmalade*, for which she won a Theatre World Award.

She has worked with her mother in films, playing her younger self in *Evening* (2007). Mamie became familiar to the American public when she played Sally Adams, the daughter-in-law of the second US President in the much-praised HBO series *John Adams*. Mamie made her Broadway debut in 2008 as the innocent Cécile Volanges in Christopher Hampton's *Les Liasons Dangeueses*. She looks very like her mother and says of her: 'She's an amazing lady. It's always been there, that shadow. It's been a comforting presence. I feel like I've negotiated how to live with it.'

Grace, who is 23 years old, began her acting career in 2008 at the Wild Project in the East Village, New York, in Neil Blackadder's *The Sexual Neuroses of Our Parents*. She played Dora, who, after 10 years on tranquilizers, develops an insatiable sexual appetite which results in an unwanted pregnancy and a grisly abortion. The play got reviews to make mother proud. 'It is really Grace Gummer's play, and she utterly commands the stage in an immaculately restrained performance. At first, she is locked inside herself, largely talked at by her family and reduced to short monotone responses. But as she leaves the numbing drugs behind, her deadpan is interrupted by her sarcastic but spot-on repetitions from the world around her, something that only serves to make her even more of a mirror. By the end of the play, she is still fairly still, but her words are more and more her own, like her needs.'

Louisa, who is 19 years old, is still a student. At the beginning of 2009 I was privy to Streep being asked by an English actress when she was going to return to the stage. 'Children like nothing more than that you are out every evening and every weekend,' she replied and went on to analyse herself:

'I was wired for family. You know how they say people are wired for religion, or wired for this or that? I always knew I would like to, if I could find the right person, have a family. I can't imagine living single, although, frankly, sometimes it's rather attractive. I think you have to have somebody as a partner who shares what you value in life. I've always loved raising a family, and Don always gets that it's a very big, important job and a hard job. A really, really hard job. And it never ends.'

Queen Victoria was pregnant for 17 years of her reign and still managed to rule an Empire. Streep has had less help but has been pregnant for three years during a tenth of her professional career; she has still managed to run that career without interruption. Both of them, strong and determined women.

Women learn how to mother often from their own mothers, according to psychologists. Streep's mother was also, as she said, her first producer. Her beloved mother died in 2001. Her father, Harry, died three years later. He was 92 and she had looked after him for the final years of his life when he needed constant care.

Good parents want their children to inherit a better and safer world.

Streep, always an active opponent of nuclear power, has become more vociferous politically. Accepting her Golden Globe for *Angels in America*, she attacked

President Bush's position on gay marriage and backstage afterwards, when asked what the biggest problem facing America was, replied: 'It has three initials.' At a Radio City Music Hall fundraiser for Senator John Kerry, she spelt out her position on the invasion of Iraq. 'During "shock and awe", I wondered which of the megaton bombs Jesus, our president's personal saviour, would have personally dropped on the sleeping families of Baghdad. I wondered, "Does Jesus understand collateral damage?" '

Even when publicising her films, she would sometimes take the opportunity to release some political polemic. Promoting the remake of *The Manchurian Candidate* (2004) in which she played the Machiavellian, ice-chewing Senator Eleanor Prentiss Shaw, Streep told the press: 'So many questions are interesting about a woman like that, a woman in power and how she's regarded. I'm fascinated by people like Margaret Thatcher and Madeleine Albright. I looked at those people, the ones who make things happen – Karen Hughes and Peggy Noonan. Their certainty. Unshakeable. People like that work all their lives to achieve these positions where they can move world events – and then they can't control them. That's my character. They get into a place where they control nothing because they never learn that the tangent is the thing that controls events.'

Streep has also lent her name to campaigns against domestic violence and Hudson River pollution. 'What pushed me over the edge? Name a topic. Everything pushed me over the edge! The quiet dismantling of environmental regulations. Everybody should be getting up and making a big fat noise. Yes, of course, I always question why anyone would listen to an actor. But it's not your profession that defines you so much as your personhood. I listen to all kinds of people whose qualifications to opine on anything are that they have a radio show or a degree in art history. Our most famous president of late was an actor. You don't jettison your citizenship because you're famous.'

Beneath her calm and controlled exterior, Streep can be a very passionate woman. When Madonna dropped out of the film *Music of the Heart* (1999), the director, Wes Craven, best known for his *Scream* films, wrote Streep an impassioned letter; he told her that for 20 years he had been trying to make a film of the true story of Roberta Guaspari-Tzavaras, who fought the Board of Education to teach music to underprivileged kids in East Harlem. She was such a brilliant teacher that some of the children ended up performing at Carnegie Hall at a fund raising event.

'Never in my life had I gotten a letter like that from a director,' Streep recalled, 'and I was seduced by his passion.' However Roberta was a violin virtuoso and Streep was not. So she asked for shooting to be postponed for eight weeks while she studied the violin under Sandy Park from the New York Philharmonic, Streep practised six hours a day.

Craven recalled the climax of the film. 'It was a night to remember. Streep was portraying Roberta Guaspari, and some of the world's greatest living violinists, including Isaac Stern and Itzhak Perlman, gave virtuoso performances. Just before this scene was shot Isaac Stern asked Streep, 'Can you play the Bach Double?' She replied that she could. So he made her come into the maestro suite and play it for him at that moment and that was just what she needed.'

Streep added: 'When I walked out on the stage, I wasn't scared, which is good, because there were 2000 extras in the audience. I was scared shitless in that room with him, but he delivered me into the scene.'

When she came to do it in public, Craven observed Stern nudge Perlman and point at Streep. Then both the maestros nodded.

The film was not a widely popular one – inner city Harlem children are not big box-office and it grossed only half of its budget – but it was an important one to get made.

When I wrote at the beginning of the book that Streep is a significant exception to William Goldman's 'Nobody knows anything' adage, it does not mean that she has a golden touch for increasing studio profits; it means that she has a nose for what scripts have quality and are worth making.

In 2006 she agreed, for just the Screen Actors' Guild minimum wage, to take the leading role in a low-budget first film by a Chinese opera director, Chen Shi-Zheng. *Dark Matter* was inspired by a tragedy: on 1 November 1991, five employees of the University of Iowa were killed, when Gang Lu, a physics graduate student, went on a shooting rampage before he committed suicide.

It was rumored that the gunman was upset because he had been denied an academic award.

Chen's production of the 19 hour Chinese opera *The Peony Pavilion* was a major cultural event in the history of the Lincoln Center. And that made it possible for him, I suspect, to get his script to Streep.

Chen recalled: 'When I brought the story to her, I said: *Dark Matter*'s parallel structure places the image of spiral galaxies and the invisible source of their movement against spiraling, escalating emotions from within; the motion within emotion, you might say. It reminded me of the poet who said the world is not made of atoms; the world is made of stories. In *Dark Matter*, cosmology serves as the story and the film becomes an exploration of how we communicate story and – more specifically in this case – how failed communication saddens the story. She agreed, totally. She felt that Americans look through a window that offers a limited view, and the story was important because it wasn't about a poor, struggling immigrant; it was about a brilliant mind that could potentially contribute to society. It wasn't a story about teenage rampage. It was about an intelligent person compelled to tragic circumstance.'

So Streep agreed to play an American who bridges the gap between East and West; Joanna Silver, a wealthy patron of Chinese culture and an unofficial counsellor to the visiting students, who takes a maternal interest in the killer.

The movie played at Redford's Sundance Festival and

was praised for its clever concept and its original style. It is divided into five chapters, each titled after a different element. The ethereal voices of the Beijing Angelic Choir, singing a cappella Chinese-language renditions of songs like 'Beautiful Dreamer' become a kind of Greek chorus underscoring the cultural divide. Excerpts from *Tosca* and *Madame Butterfly* are incisively used as plot pointers.

But then disaster struck. Two separate attacks on 16 April 2007, took place on the campus of Virginia Polytechnic Institute and the State University in Blacksburg, Virginia. The perpetrator, Seung-Hui Cho, killed 32 people and wounded many others before committing suicide. No single gunman in the history of the United States has ever shot more victims in one burst. The film, an intelligent inquiry into the mind of such a man was never properly released. *Dark Matter* didn't even open in the UK.

14

Devils in Disguise

I once spent a pleasant Sunday with Anna Wintour at the Greenwich Village apartment of our mutual friend, Gully. Anna seemed a slight reserved and rather posh girl – her grandfather was a major-general and her father, Charles Vere Wintour (Oundle, Cambridge and the Garrick Club) – was a distinguished newspaper editor. Her step-mother, Audrey Slaughter, founder of the popular teenage magazines *Honey* and *Petticoat* fanned the flames of young Anna's interest in fashion journalism. She became editor of *American Vogue* and I later couldn't believe the things I read about her – imperious, ruthless, fearsome: *Nuclear Wintour*. It was true that she had a rather frightening helmet of hair and was always pictured in dark glasses at fashion shows, backing into the limelight in the front row. I asked Gully if any of this was true. She bashfully admitted that Anna did get up at 6 a.m. to have 'quality time' with her children before work.

A bright young graduate called Laura Weisberger got a job as Anna's assistant at *American Vogue*, but quit after ten months because she felt 'out of place'. The following year she published a book, *The Devil Wears Prada*, about Andy, a bright young graduate who went through fashion hell as the assistant to Miranda Priestly – the imperious, ruthless, fearsome editor of a fashion magazine.

According to Laura, the character wasn't based on Anna. 'While I didn't necessarily begin writing with the intent of creating a 'boss from hell' story, it's obviously a large component of the book,' she said. 'A lot of the anecdotes and demands and craziness are products of my imagination, stories I created at four in the morning while chugging coffee and fighting sleep deprivation. But there's reality there, too. Some of the stories aren't so far away from the tasks either I or my friends in various industries – whether fashion or magazines or PR or advertising – went through in our first few years out of college. I imagine that assistants everywhere will recognize some of their own experiences in Andy's life.'

The producer, Wendy Finerman, who had built her reputation in Hollywood on *Forrest Gump* (1994), had her golden retrievers stalking the streets of New York in search of truffles and they sniffed out a succulent one in this 'not-the-Anna-Wintour' story. They snapped it up long before it was published and became a New York Times best-seller. Wendy's 'Gump' star Tom Hanks had produced a popular television series 'From the Earth to the Moon' about all the Apollo missions and one of the directors, David Frankel, had gone on to make *Sex and the City*. Wendy hired him and they went through a posse of writers trying to get the project sleek enough to present to Streep. The final draft attracted Streep with a role that was crueller than Cruela De Vil, the devil-woman who makes coats from the fur of puppies.

Whatever the provenance of the project, Streep had no intention of basing her character on Wintour. Although her clothes were, inevitably, Prada, they fell just a little short of the outrageous and her hair was an aggressive bomb-proof silvery grey swoop. Streep said: 'I'm sort of a notorious pain in the butt for any costume designer because I have so many opinions about how my people should present.' She went on to explain: 'I feel very strongly that we make decisions about what we're giving to the world or what we're withholding from the world by virtue of what we put on our bodies and what we choose to say and not say. So for me clothes are kind of the character.'

Streep frequently complains that, in the male ethos of Hollywood, there are so few scripts made which have strong women's parts but, ironically, in the case of Miranda Priestly, she looked for role models not in any women but in men. She explains:

'Most of the people whom I have come across who wield power and great realms of influence are male. It's much more fun for me to make the über boss out of my own pastiche of experience ... so that's what I did. I was interested in making a human being as contradictory and messy as we all are. I think that's she's an exacting, highly disciplined, demanding,

191

ambitious person who doesn't necessarily take the time for all the nice social lubricants that help make the workplace graceful and fun. But, compared to the people that I know, Miranda's so well behaved. She's almost like a diplomat compared to some men who are very, very powerful in our business.'

One dreads to think who these people are Streep has mixed with. Do they demand their assistant get two copies of the next 'Harry Potter' novel which hasn't even been punished? Do they summon her to their New York office and order her to make a restaurant reservation without letting her know the restaurant is in Washington? Do they give her the sadistic task of getting her to inform her superior, who loves going to the Paris fashion shows, that she won't be going ... but she (the assistant) will? Do they order her to 'find the piece of paper I had in my hand yesterday morning' or tell her how much they regret hiring 'smart, fat girls'?

I would venture to suggest that, as written, Miranda exceeds any known male executive in terms of cruelty, largely because she sets out to torture Andy and succeeds with aplomb. It makes for an original and wickedly funny film with exchanges such as:

Miranda: 'You have no sense of fashion...'
Andy: 'I think that depends on...'
Miranda: 'No, no, that wasn't a question.'

Or:

Miranda: 'I need ten or fifteen skirts from Calvin Klein.'
Andy: 'What kind of skirts?'
Miranda: 'Please, bore someone else with your questions.'

Just as the Devil has all the best tunes, scathing Miranda has all the best lines. Unfortunately for Anne Hathaway who plays the put-upon Andy, this means she has such a supplicant part that she is only visible when her bovine eyes are caught in the headlights of Miranda's spleen. To make matters worse Andy is saddled with a boyfriend chef who is lingeringly uninteresting – better to be tongue lashed by Miranda than on the receiving end of anything from him.

Streep bestrides 'Prada' like a colossus, dominating the movie with the pinpoint power of her performance. Many critics said she was the only reason to see the film, and millions did. It was an unexpected worldwide hit for Twentieth Century Fox turning its $35 million cost into ten times that at the international box office, making it Streep's most commercially successful movie to date.

'Miranda is a person who lives to work – there's a little bit of that in me,' she observed. More than a little, possibly. But Miranda keeps on losing husbands, which Streep most certainly has not.

Curiously, for Streep, the film wasn't that much fun to make. 'Everyone asks "Oh, was it so much fun?" No, it was not fun to be this person. I didn't stay in character when they yelled cut but I was in a sort of self-induced bad mood all the time. When you're a controlling task-master, everything is not quite right. Generally you're dissatisfied and that state of being is not wholly enjoyable. So I found that I couldn't enter into this fun on the set because I felt it wouldn't help the dynamic if I immediately went over and was joking with Emily and Anne and Stanley Tucci. They all were always having a party in the corner and I just couldn't join in. It was sort of a lonely position that I staked out for myself but I suppose it paid off ultimately.'

'Weeks before we begin shooting, the company starts to get together. Whoever is playing Meryl's lover is in love with her. Whoever is playing the villain is a little afraid of her. And whoever is playing her best friend is her best friend. She shifts her soul slightly and changes the chemistry of all the relationships.'

Anna Wintour attended a press preview of the film, where Streep met her for the first time, and said that she found it 'amusing'.

Purposefully Streep made Miranda very soft-spoken. It was an astute decision. 'In my experience really powerful people don't have to raise their voice,' she noted. 'In fact the less they raise their voice, the more people are scared of them.'

It was a timbre that she kept for her part as the CIA operative, Corinne Whitman, in *Rendition* the following year. Clad in smooth silk evening gowns, she speaks her robotic, neocon lines in a soft Southern drawl. It makes her character twice as frightening, with the morality of Richard III – 'Conscience is a word that cowards use ... I can smile and murder while I smile.'

This was never going to be a multiplex movie in the United States as it addressed the CIA practice of flying terrorist suspects to countries where the government knew they would be tortured to extract information. Jake Gyllenhaal is a CIA Agent obliged to watch an innocent Egptian-born American undergo this sickening activity. He implores his boss to bring it to an end. Corinne Whitman, head of CIA anti-terrorist operations, counters his plea with the justification: 'Honey, this is a nasty business. There are upwards of 7,000 people in central London alive tonight because of information that we elicited just this way. So maybe you can put your head on your pillow and feel proud for saving one man while 7,000 perish, but I got grandkids in London, so I'm glad I'm doing this job ... and you're not.'

Rendition is an overtly political film which does little to dispel the common misapprehension that Extraordinary Rendition was another evil act of the Bush regime. In fact, the CIA started flying Al Quaeda suspects to Egypt while Clinton was President and with his knowledge. It escalated after 9/11 and the establishment of Guantanomo Bay as Vice-President Dick Cheney asking Congress to exempt CIA officials from legislation that prevented political prisoners being subject to cruel and degrading treatment.

Whether the movie had any effect on rendition is improbable. Only one million of the USA's 300 million citizens bothered to go and see it. Streep took the part, she said, because of the even-handedness of the script, as ever seeing the story through her, admittedly smallish, role. 'I feel compassion for people who choose to stand up and be public servants and take responsibility for people around the world.'

Well-intentioned movies that play to small houses are not good career moves usually. Tom Cruise had lost much of his credibility in the USA after jumping up and down on a sofa on *The Oprah Winfrey Show* to proclaim his love for Katie Holmes, a replacement for Nicole Kidman. Cruise created more ripples by then going on NBC's *Today Show* to reprimand Brooke Shields for taking medication to alleviate her post-partum depression, something prohibited by that well-known mind-bender, L. Ron Hubbard, father of the Church of Scientology. This upset Paula Fortunato, 43, the wife of 83-year-old Sumner Redstone, the Viacom chairman and owner of Paramount, who announced that Tom's behaviour was 'not acceptable to the studio'.

Cruise's partner in his unrenewed bread-and-breakfast deal at Paramount was his former agent, Paula Wagner, who was married to Rick Nicita, one of the managing partners of Streep's agency, Creative Artists. They were hardly going to let the superstar's career be wrecked, so, to save face, Wagner and Cruise took over the largely defunct United Artists studio. To get the show on the road they made a film *Lions for Lambs* (2007) and called in the services of the man who in many ways got Creative Artists off the ground, Robert Redford.

He was to direct and another favoured client, Meryl Streep, was to star.

To say that it was an unformed script panicked into production would be generous. Redford, turned 70, still looked presentable but was not as dab a hand as directing as he had when he won the Oscar for *Ordinary People* in 1980. *Lions for Lambs* was a quote from a German general during the First World War regarding the British politicians view of their foot soldiers – although not one on the lips of every American.

The story takes place concurrently in three locations: in Afghanistan two young Army rangers are injured and stranded behind the lines; in Washington, an ambitious young senator (Tom Cruise) unveils his new Middle East strategy to a television reporter (Meryl Streep); in California, a political science professor (Robert Redford) tries to convince a gifted student not to devote his life to money and pleasure, but to devote it to his country.

Streep did her energetic and enthusiastic best but, after *Rendition* and now this, she maybe wondered if her days of juicy leading roles were coming to an end.

If she did, happily, she was wrong.

15

Beauty and the Beast

In March 1923, a reporter from The New York Times asked the British mountaineer George Leigh Mallory why he wanted to climb Mount Everest. Mallory paused, thought about it and then replied: 'Because it's there.'

The same could be said of why Streep wanted to play the lead in the movie of *Mamma Mia!* (2008). It had been a walloping hit of a stage musical with a worldwide gross of over $2 billion in 33 countries, playing to an estimated audience of more than 30 million people and rising.

The producer Judy Craymer, after working on Tim Rice's *Chess* with the Abba composers, Bjorn Ulvaeus and Benny Anderson, had the hunch that their established hits would make a more popular musical than the one they had just written. Possibly she was inspired by the insight of Bobby Gillespie of Primal Scream who pronounced of Abba: 'The songs manage to combine a melancholic feeling with a euphoric feeling. That is interesting and true because the songs are very often in minor keys and the lyrics are very often sad, but still the sound is uplifting.' Or maybe she just liked the tunes.

The Swedish group used to be known as Agnetha, Benny, Bjorn and Anni-frid, but this became a bit of a mouthful as their reputation grew so they reduced it to the acronym ABBA. Only B and B wrote the songs and music and they resisted Craymer tampering with their art and would only agree to the use of their work if she came up with a plot which was worthy of them. After a couple of rejected attempts, she was introduced to Catherine Johnston, a 'Bush Baby' who wrote plays for the small Bush Theatre in West London and was in the process of developing 'Shang-a-Lang' about the 40th birthday weekend of three women who head for Butlins to try to relive the Bay City Rollers fantasies of their youth. Pauline is determined to have a birthday to remember (or, possibly, forget), Jackie is there to try to restrain her and Lauren is a burnt-out drunk.

Craymer and Johnston might well have had in their mutual subconscious the film, co-written by Dennis Norden, *Bueno Sera, Mrs Campbell* (1964) in which Italian villager Gina Lollobrigida has lived off paternity payments coughed up by three GI's – Telly Savalas, Peter Lawford and Phil Silvers – pretending to each of them that her appropriately named daughter, Gia, was theirs. Twenty years later the three GI's return to the village for a reunion...

Switch from Italy to Greece where Gia has become Sophie. She is going to get married and wants Daddy to lead her down the aisle. Fortunately her hippy mother, Donna, has recorded her bonks from the summer of love twenty years previously in her diary and along come the three possible dads. Her mother has invited the other two members of her erstwhile singing troupe, Donna and the Dynamos, to the wedding and, at the drop of a drop of Ouzo, they are apt to burst into song.

Phyllida Lloyd, who had done everything from TV drama to *La Bohème*, was signed to direct *Mamma Mia!*

The movie didn't begin to materialize until 2007 and younger names than Streep's (who would be 58 when they started to shoot) were in the frame for the lead role of Donna Sheridan – Nicole Kidman, Michelle Pfeiffer, Kim Basinger, but, thankfully, not Madonna.

As soon as the London show was hailed as a hit in 1999 Craymer, had been courted by three of the major studios, all of them – not so coincidentally – with women at the helm: Elizabeth Gabler at Fox, Stacy Snider at Universal and Sherry Lansing at Paramount. But, wisely, she held onto the film rights until she was in a strong enough position to call all the shots; she had done that with the stage show and that had gone rather splendidly and so, she reasoned, she could do it again with the movie.

There lurked in the wings a dangerous precedent: the film version of *The Phantom of the Opera* (2004). Andrew Lloyd Webber had a stage hit of *Mia* proportions but, in choosing to produce the film version personally, he made errors: the script by himself and the director, Joel Schumacher, had no real drama or menace and the casting of Emmy Possum (*As the World Turns*) and Gerard Butler (former president of Glasgow University

Law Society) was a false economy – he needed stars. And Joel Schumacher was a director who swamped any drama with design, reminding the world that he started out in life as a window-dresser on Fifth Avenue. The movie was not the intended hit that Disney had hoped for.

But Judy Craymer was undaunted and Meryl Streep has a lot to thank her for. In the face of studio executives who were suggesting Kylie Minogue for the part of Donna, she knew she needed a supreme actress to give the fairy tale a spine and a big name so that she could 'cast up' the other roles. So, after Universal had been persuaded to meet Creative Artists's asking price for the star, Kevin Huvane telephoned her when she was driving along in her BMW through the wooded farmland of Connecticut and told her the deal was done. She whooped: 'I *am* Mamma Mia'. Perhaps, it should have been 'I *am* Momma Mia' since she and her daughter would become American in the film.

At a London press conference a journalist had the temerity to suggest Streep had written to the New York production indicating she would rather like to be in a movie of the show if it ever happened. She sighed. 'This story is completely untrue. What I did was to take my ten-year-old daughter and her friends to the stage show seven years ago. We were dancing in the aisles and down the street afterwards so I wrote the cast a 'mash' note.' (The expression a 'mash note' has long fallen out of use in the UK. It used to mean a letter from a stranger to someone who was unlikely to reciprocate their affection. But in Meryl's time at university it was an expression for someone having a crush on another.)

Streep's letter reached and remained with the show's creator, Judy Craymer, who, a year earlier, revealed it contained the broad hint: 'I would love to know what it would be like to get up on the stage and be part of *Mamma Mia*.' One wonders why Streep is so touchy on the subject; after all Sir John Gielgud, when unemployed, used to write letters to all the major theatre producers, seeking work.

Streep's casting meant they could attract Pierce Brosnan, the man who resuscitated the James Bond franchise, as Donna's foremost former lover. 'I went to see the show in London before we started filming,' 007 confessed, 'and I thought, 'Oh my God, what have I said yes to?' But I kept repeating 'Meryl Streep's doing it, Meryl Streep's doing it' to calm myself down. That was my mantra. But actually I enjoyed working for women. There's less of the bluff and bluster of the male ego that sometimes happens.'

There was sufficient in the budget to afford Pierce but evidently not enough to afford to give him singing lessons: his voice proved shaky rather than stirring. He did have one moment of genuine panic at the end of the nine-week shoot at Pinewood when he was dressed in a body-hugging, spangled, Spandex, blue flared outfit, his hair in an Elvis quiff. As the assistant director led him to the sound stage for the final song, 'Waterloo', he suddenly realised that Bond had started shooting at the same studio that week. 'Fuck, what if I bump into Daniel Craig?' he shivered.

The name Streep also attracted Colin Firth, the pin-up British actor who had played a masterful Mr Darcy to Elizabeth Bennett in the BBC series of Jane Austen's *Pride and Prejudice* and again, sportingly, to a plumped up Renee Zellweger in two films taken from *Bridget Jones Diary'*. Had he really fathered little Sophie in the Swinging Sixties it would have been something of a feat since Colin was only ten by the end of that decade but, in movies, all things are possible – in Mel Gibson's *Hamlet* (1990) Glenn Close as Gertrude must have given birth to the prince at the even more tender age of nine.

Some commentators felt it was a mistake for the screen's finest actor to dignify this pop-romp with her participation. But Streep had no doubts. 'It's a requirement of popular culture that you strike an ironic distance. This doesn't. It's a film about women and their whole experiences being hopeful and youthful and older and suffering the regrets that you have over a long life. It's visceral and I love that. At one point, when Donna took her shirt off, I wanted there to be tattoos all up and down. They convinced me that was too much. I wanted to wear her past on a body that was already middle-aged. I wanted to have a little road map where you are reading who she was. Women especially read all those clues really, really closely.'

The other two Dynamos were played by comic actresses of a similar age – a padded Julie Walters (Mrs Weasley in Harry Potter) and the lank Christine Baranski

204

made up the trio with brio. 'If you thought we were having a ball, we were,' said Streep. 'There was absolutely no acting involved.'

Lithe and active, she did indeed do the splits against a blue screen but when another unfortunate reporter at the London press conference asked her if she had done all her stunts she countered: 'Do you think they pasted my head on somebody else's body?' So we must assume she scaled a 40-foot goat house, tumbled through a roof, slid down a banister and cannon-balled into the sea herself – presumably while the nine credited stunt doubles sat and played cards, probably with the film's insurers

What she did do was to sing and dance exuberantly and earn the respect of Phyllida Lloyd. 'She's a fantastic collaborator. She'll offer you twenty ways to do the scene. She is a gift for a director. I would walk over broken glass for her.'

The film can be faulted on various technical aspects – the fact that they shot studio interiors first and then went to the glorious Greek islands mismatches the feel and the light – but nobody goes away from such a movie singing the scenery. It's fun – and so was Streep's approach. 'Who wouldn't want to have the chance of kissing James Bond? I felt I was doing it for all of America, for all the women. It's just one of the perks of the job.'

Streep, as ever, was sensitive to any criticism of the movie, referring in an interview to 'Englishmen of the pundit class who wrote about the film. The vitriol! Just

205

columns and columns of high-brow rage. So much of movie-going is a willingness to enter in and they will never enter into *Mamma Mia*. Just like I will never enter into that Tarantino world, ever. I'm just never going to laugh when someone has their brains splattered along the front of the windscreen. But I sit in a theatre in Manhattan and all the cognoscenti, the hippest people in New York, are roaring. "Mamma" is a benign thing. It's not loathsome. It's not putting crap in the world.'

In fact most of the better British critics joined in the fun – indeed Hugo Rifkind, writing in *The Times*, went as far as to say 'Streep is the real star here, and she does serious acting, too, investing a cliff-top rendition of "The Winner Takes It All" with far more teary gravitas than should be possible for a song that contains the line: "I figured it made sense/building me a fence".' But not Rex Reed in *The New York Observer*; he seemed positively offended. 'To me, the popularity of the jukebox blather of this gang of no-talents is only slightly less understandable than the war in Iraq.' He received an avalanche of venom from his readers for this.

Streep was only too aware that this film, above all others, was critic-proof. 'I know the studio is gobsmacked by its success and a lot of the critics have been surprised, but I wasn't. It was a no brainer. I knew it would do well because it was aimed at an audience that has been neglected in recent years in film offerings: women. They are the last group anybody ever cares about.' With a worldwide gross of $575,000,000 plus a DVD sale of $120,000,000 and rising at the time of writing, *Mamma*

Mia! will have Meryl, Judy and Phyllida singing 'Money! Money! Money!' for the rest of their lives.

One can imagine Streep metaphorically licking her lips as she cast aside the baggy blue jeans of Donna in order to exchange them, a few weeks later, for the austere bonnet and habit of Sister Aloysius in *Doubt* (2008). She threw away the outfit and put on the years, about thirty of them, to portray the hatchet-faced, thin-lipped nun, pink eyes snarling below interrogator's spectacles, who rules her Catholic school by fear, instilled not just into the pupils but the staff as well.

John Patrick Shanley's play had opened on Broadway in 2004 and won a clutch of Tonys and a Pulitzer Prize. Set in the Bronx in 1964, it addressed the conundrum of whether St Nicholas's priest, Father Flynn, did or didn't have improper relations with a young black male student. Sister Aloysius has no doubts that he did, even confronting Flynn with the phrase: 'I have my certainty.'

She tricks him into resigning by pretending she has the drop on him from a nun at his previous parish. It's a lie but 'In the pursuit of wrongdoing, one steps away from God.' 'Did you ever prove it?' the innocent Sister James asks her at the end. 'To whom?' comes the reply. 'Anybody but yourself,' says the young woman. Sister Aloysius at last unbends and then confesses: 'I have doubts. I have such terrible doubts.'

I asked Shanley why he cast Streep and his reply was not wholly informative: 'If you were in a subway carriage and asked thirty people who should play Sister Aloysius, they would all say Meryl Streep.' I suspect a more candid answer might have been: 'In order to get a four-handed, entirely verbal play made into a movie.' It would appear that the producer, Scott Rudin, whose production company made *Marvin's Room* with Rober De Niro's company and *The Hours* for Miramax and now *Doubt* for the same studio, seems to have moved in as producer-in-residence to Streep since he is also making her next two films. Once he had signed the character actor of the moment, Philip Seymour Hoffman (who had played Konstantin in Streep's *Seagull* in the Park in 2001) to lock horns with Sister Aloysius as Father Flynn, the project flew. Shanley added that Hoffman was the only actor he could think of who could 'make Meryl sweat' through every scene of *Doubt*. From where I sat, the reverse seemed the case.

Streep spent time with the nuns at the College of Mount St Vincent, a Catholic liberal arts college in the Bronx. A 96-year-old nun, who ran the diocese's school system in the early 1960s, offered the actress some valuable insight into nuns during that time. 'She had a gigantic responsibility, and that was something, but she was subservient to the parish priest. You'll never see a woman celebrating Mass. There are no female mullahs. There's no female Dalai Lama,' the actress rightly observed.

Streep warmed to Shanley's thesis. 'That's the way we are – we make snap judgments about each other. There's also a visual power in this kind of paring away of everything except the encounter of human beings. Just take everything away but the light and the faces

208

and the hands. Everybody's wearing black. It's gorgeous. It's a van Dyck.'

Evidently they rehearsed for three weeks – it can't have taken that much longer to shoot – and Streep had the chance for some input. 'She made some new choices,' Shanley revealed. 'She did the big one where the accused priest asks her if she has ever committed a mortal sin and she, suddenly, is stricken and basically confessed. And I said: 'That works. I never thought of that."

Doubt was rapturously received by the acting profession with the Screen Actors Guild nominating all four leading players – Streep, Hoffman, Amy Adams and Viola Davis, who plays the mother of the possibly abused pupil – plus one for the entire cast for their ensemble – and giving the Streep the Award ahead of Kate Winslet. Not all the press were that enthusiastic. The ghost of Pauline Kael came back to haunt the film in *The New Yorker*: 'Collectors of large narrative signposts will spend a couple of happy hours at Shanley's movie, enjoying the window-rattling thunderstorms that he uses to indicate spiritual crisis, and the grimness with which Sister Aloysius, narrowing her red-rimmed eyes, delivers the line, "So, it's happened." I didn't know you could hiss, groan and murmur at the same time, but Streep can do anything.'

The New York Times was less in awe of her powers – 'Shanley's work with the actors is generally fine, though it's a mystery what he thought Ms Streep, with her wild eyes and an accent as wide as the Grand Concourse, was doing. Her outsize performance has a whiff of burlesque, but she's really just operating in a different register from the other actors, who are working in the more naturalistic vein of modern movie realism. She's a hoot, but she's also a relief, because, for some of us, worshiping Our Lady of Accents is easier on the soul than doing time in church.'

Do critics really believe that a Streep performance is something conjured up or controlled by a director – especially in his first film? On matters of script, however, especially lines which are not hers, Streep didn't win every argument. In an interview with *The Daily Telegraph* she revealed a rehearsal row of 'knock- down, drag-out' proportions with Rudin about a new scene Shanley had inserted in the movie version. 'I wasn't angry, I was speechless. Because I don't really think that doubt in increments should be removed from this at all. Doubt is our friend. And once you tip the scales in one direction or another it's very, very dangerous. The thing is calibrated like a tuning fork: it's either A or it's not A.' She almost told them that if the scene stayed she would stay at home and do no publicity. 'That, by the way, is the only thing they pay attention to. Not "I think this", "I feel very strongly about that" – that's just noise. But I didn't have a prayer.'

The article forbore to say which scene it was so I asked Shanley which one. He was amused. 'She was coy, was she? It was Flynn's farewell sermon. You need closure, you need to see him go.' In it the good or bad Father tells a packed congregation that, as in all our lives, there is a wind that is taking us in a certain

210

direction, in his case away from them. And the wind is driven by a power with a superior knowledge as to what is for the best.

Streep's opposition to this apparent softening of a man whom Sister Aloysius was sure was a paedophile was yet another instance of her arguing the corner of her character. 'A friend Gavin de Becker, a security consultant, wrote a book called *The Gift of Fear*. It was about women's intuition, just basically saying if you sense that something's off, if you feel unsafe, you probably are – on some level. You're not paranoid; you're probably right. We're animals. We smell it. We smell danger and I think that Sister Aloysius senses something. Whether it's from something she knows from deep, deep in her past. She knows what it is. She's seen this before. I sympathised with her plight, with where she found herself in this world.'

But the fact is: Sister Aloysius wasn't real; she was a pawn in a drama, as much as Joanna Kramer or Sophie Zawistowski. Shanley could see where Streep was coming from. 'She's an actor. And she's inside the story. And no matter how she protests and how she struggles, she is going to inhabit a point of view which is not the point of view of the film but of a character in the film.'

Unwittingly he had put his finger precisely on what distinguishes Meryl Streep and has made her first among equals. She isn't part of the film; the film is part of her. When she has a commanding role, she subtly commands the film. In films like *Out of Africa* and *The*

211

Bridges of Madison County, the Streep character narrates the story. But – and this is her art – even when she isn't narrating the story, she is. With her voice, her eyes, her mouth, every bit of body movement, her very presence she is storytelling just as surely as she might tell it with words.

Streep has her own doubts. After her early experiences in *Holocaust* and *Sophie's Choice* she found it hard to believe in a conventional God. But when she received her Lifetime Achievement Award from the American Film Institute she seemed quite spiritual: 'I want to thank some people who aren't here. They couldn't be because they're in heaven. I want to thank my mother and father, the funniest, saddest, most musical, gorgeous, weird, strong personalities. They fought with each other for sixty years and taught me everything I know about drama.'

She had been wary about accepting the Award at what was traditionally an over-the-top ceremony and discussed the prospect with Al Pacino. 'Some parts of us are very shy in terms of that kind of attention,' he agreed. She shook her head, almost regretting what she was letting herself in for. 'And we get plenty of it We get so much attention. My God. I mean, that's the problem. You know, I love what I do and I've been very, very well rewarded for it, and this is a great honor, but I can't help thinking . . .' And there she sighed.

But she needn't have worried. I have rarely seen her happier as she sat, in a flowing black gown topped by a crisp white shirt with upturned collar, at a table bedecked with roses, surrounded by Don and the children as they listened to the fulsome tributes that flowed from Clint Eastwood, Robert De Niro, Al Pacino, Jack Nicholson, Mike Nichols, Goldie Hawn, Shirley MacClaine, Diane Keaton, Kevin Kline, Nora Ephron, James Woods and ... and, if Hollywood has royalty, they were all there that night.

Meryl alternately clutched her son and her husband as the waves of superlatives flew towards her, sometimes very close to tears, at others exultant with laughter, especially when Jim Carey, with whom she had worked in *Lemony Snicket's A Series of Unfortunate Events* informed the assembled luminaries: 'I didn't know what she'd be like but luckily for me she was open and willing to learn. Remember that scene where you were all over the place, eating the damn scenery and hamming it up. I said. "Hey, Meryl – less is more" and you picked right up on it.'

He then left the stage and approached her, bursting into a rendition of The Beatles'song, plaintive and melodic, 'All You Need is Love' –

There's nothing you can do that can't be done.
Nothing you can sing that can't be sung.
All you need is love.

And certainly the praise and love showered on Streep by her peers transcended the usual Hollywood hyperbole. When she finally picked up the Award, she told them: 'I wish I were her, I really do.'

Her parents apart, one other person who couldn't be there was Joe Papp of the New York Public Theater who discovered Meryl and was her early mentor. I was fortunate enough to talk to him about her shortly before he died. He deserves to have the penultimate word because, maybe, he is her Angel. 'She has a deep social conscience. She's well informed and she cares about the world, getting involved in movements that address the nuclear threat. At the same time she has a marvelous sense of humour. She's like a kid when she gets happy, larking around like a twelve-year-old. She can be a determined actress to work with in terms of doing it her way. She shapes the role in terms of her own sensibilities and intelligence, which is very high. A director cannot make an off-the-cuff remark about how he wants things, she'll zero right in on it. Not that she's perfect. She can be tough and a pain in the ass like anybody else. But, essentially, she's a decent and honest person.'

And Streep on Streep? 'Let's face it, we were all once three-year-olds who stood in the middle of the living room and everybody thought we were so adorable. Only some of us grow up and get paid for it.'

Afterword

Heartfelt thanks: to those people in the film industry who shared their memories of working with Meryl Streep; to my researchers, Jacina Coyne, Anna Maconochie and Tivian Zvekan, for their cheerful diligence; to Michael Carson for his thoughtful editing; to my agent, Sonia Lang, for getting this book off the ground and to David Cohen, who was more than a publisher but a font of original ideas and philosophical wisdom. My wife, Mo, was a knowledgeable sounding board and my son, Oliver, created the right atmosphere in the house since he is at drama school and the smell of grease-paint is more inspirational than incense when you're writing a book about an actor.

It never occurred to me to ask Meryl Streep if I might do an authorized book. That would be something entirely different, looking at her body of work from her point of view, not mine. I recalled the principle of Quantum Theory, namely that if a body knows it is being watched, the observer effects the subject's behaviour. But my thanks to her anyway; she has made such stimulating choices in her career that it was more than stimulating

215

to analyse her work and try to find out what makes Streep Streep.

Iain Johnstone.
February 2009

Filmography

Secret Service (1977) (TV)

Director: Peter Levin, Screenplay: William Gillette. Producer Ken Campbell. Meryl Streep (Edith Varney), Lenny Baker (Henry Dumont), Frederick Coffin (Lt Maxwell), Alice Drummond (Mrs Varney).

Streep plays a local girl used to trap a Union spy in Richmond, Virginia in October 1864.

117 mins. (Phoenix Theatre, Public Broadcasting Service (PBS))

The Deadliest Season (1977) (TV)

Director: Robert Markowitz, Screenplay: Ernest Kinoy, Producer: Robert Berger. Meryl Streep (Sharon Miller), Michael Moriarty (Gerry Miller), Kevin Conway (George Graff), Sully Boyer (Tom Feeney).

Michael Moriarty plays ice hockey player Gerry Miller. Under pressure to be more successful, he adopts an aggressive style on the ice and is charged with manslaughter after a member of the opposing team dies. In her first ever film appearance, Streep plays the hockey player's wife.

98 mins. (Titus Productions)

217

Julia (1977)

Director: Fred Zinnemann, Novel by Lillian Hellman, Screenplay: Alvin Sargent, Producer: Richard Roth. Meryl Streep (Anne Marie), Jane Fonda (Lillian Hellman), Vanessa Redgrave (Julia), Jason Robards (Dashiell Hammett)

Sporting a black wig, Streep plays Anne Marie, the bitchy friend of playwright Lillian Hellman.

118 mins. (20th Century Fox)

Holocaust (1978)

Director: Marvin J. Chomsky, Screenplay: Gerald Green, Producer: Robert Berger. Meryl Streep (Inga Helms Weiss), James Woods (Karl Weiss), Michael Moriarty (Erik Dorf), Rosemary Harris (Berta Palitz Weiss).

Streep plays a German woman whose Jewish husband is taken to a concentration camp. The film follows each member of the Weiss family as they struggle to survive the atrocities of Nazi Germany.

Awards: Outstanding Lead Actress in a Limited Series: Meryl Streep.

475 mins. (Titus Productions)

The Deer Hunter (1978)

Director: Michael Cimino, Screenplay: Deric Washburn, Producers: Michael Cimino, Michael Deeley, John Peverall, Barry Spikings. Meryl Streep (Linda), Robert De Niro (Michael), John Cazale (Stan), Christopher Walken (Nick), John Savage (Steven).

Nick (Walken), Michael (De Niro) and Steven (Savage) are best-friends from a small Pennsylvanian industrial town who enlist to fight in the Vietnam war. The men's lives are changed forever

218

by the war and Michael returns home to be with Nick's girlfriend, Linda (Streep) after Nick kills himself in the famous Russian roulette scene.

Awards: Best Actress in a Supporting Role: Meryl Streep. Golden Globe Nominations, Best Motion picture Actress in a Supporting Role: Meryl Streep.

182 mins. (EMI films & Universal)

Manhattan (1979)

Director: Woody Allen, Screenplay: Woody Allen & Marshall Brickman, Producer: Charles H. Joffe. Woody Allen (Isaac Davis), Diane Keaton (Mary Wilkie), Michael Murphy (Yale Pollack), Mariel Hemingway (Tracy), Meryl Streep (Jill Davis).

Streep (Jill) lives with a woman after being divorced by Woody Allen (Issac). She's writing a book that will detail some very personal secrets about their marriage. This is one of the funniest Woody Allen comedies.

96 mins. (Jack Rollins & Charles H. Joffe Productions)

The Seduction of Joe Tynan (1979)

Director: Jerry Schatzberg, Screenplay: Alan Alda, Producer: Martin Bregman. Meryl Streep: (Karen Traynor), Alan Alda:(Joe Tynan), Barbara Harris (Ellie Tynan), Rip Torn (Senator Kittner).

Streep plays the lobbyist-mistress of Alan Alda's Liberal senator in a political satire that explores the moral dilemmas on Capitol Hill.

107 mins. (Universal Pictures)

Kramer vs Kramer (1979)

Director: Robert Benton, Novel by: Avery Corman, Screenplay: Robert Benton, Producer Stanley R. Jaffe, Meryl Streep (Joanna Kramer), Dustin Hoffman (Ted Kramer), Jane Alexander (Margaret Phelps), Justin Henry (Billy Kramer).

Joanna Kramer (Streep) leaves her husband (Hoffman) and son (Justin Henry) to fend for themselves when she feels close to suicidal. They divorce and a bitter custody battle ensues.

Awards: Academy Awards won, Best Actress in a Supporting Role: Meryl Streep. Golden Globes won, Best Motion Picture Actress in a Supporting Role: Meryl Streep.

105 mins. (Columbia Pictures)

Kiss Me, Petruchio (1981) (TV)

Director: Christopher Dixon, Meryl Streep (Katherine), Raul Julia (Petruchio).

A filmed and short version of Shakespeare's 'Taming of the Shrew'.

58 mins. (PBS)

The French Lieutenant's Woman (1981)

Director: Karel Reisz, Novel by John Fowles, Screenplay: Harold Pinter, Producer: Leon Clore. Meryl Streep (Sarah/Anna), Jeremy Irons (Charles Henry Smithson/Mike), Hilton McRae (Sam), Emily Morgan (Mary).

It is 1867 in Victorian England. Streep is the beautiful woman chastised by society for having an affair with a French Lieutenant, attracting the romantic interest of Irons. There is also a film within a film in which Streep and Irons play modern day

220

equivalents, have an affair and comment on their own historical counterparts.

Awards: Academy Award Nominations, Best Actress: Meryl Streep. Golden Globes Won, Best Motion Picture Actress-Drama: Meryl Streep.

124 mins. (United Artists)

Alice At The Palace (1982) (TV)

Director: Emile Ardolino, Novel by: Lewis Carroll, Screenplay: Elizabeth Swados, Producer: Joseph Papp. Meryl Streep (Alice), Betty Aberlin (Alice's Sister), Debbie Allen (Red Queen), Richard Cox (Mad Hatter).

Streep plays the young Alice in Wonderland in this musical adaptation of the Lewis Carroll classic.

72 mins. (NBC)

Still Of The Night (1982)

Director: Robert Benton, Screenplay: Robert Benton, Producer: Arlene Donovan, Meryl Streep (Brooke Reynolds), Roy Scheider (Doctor Sam Rice), Jessica Tandy (Grace Rice), Joe Grifiasi (Joseph Vitucci).

In this Hitchcockesque thriller, Streep plays a *femme fatale*. Scheider's psychiatrist falls for her when he investigates the murder of a patient who was having an affair with Streep.

93 mins. (Metro-Goldwyn-Mayer)

Sophie's Choice (1982)

Director: Alan J. Pakula, Novel by: William Styron, Screenplay: Alan J. Pakula, Producers: Keith Barish & Alan J. Pakula. Meryl Streep (Sophie Zawistowski), Kevin Kline (Nathan Landau), Peter MacNicol (Stingo), Rita Karin (Yetta).

Streep plays Sophie, a survivor from Auschwitz, now living in Brooklyn. Her history is told in a series of flashbacks, the pinnacle of which is the famous scene in which she must make the 'choice' of which of her children to give up to the Nazis and which one to keep.

Awards: Academy Awards won, Best Actress in a Leading Role: Meryl Streep. Golden Globes won, Best Actress in a Motion Picture-Drama: Meryl Streep.

150 mins. (ITC)

Silkwood (1983)

Director: Mike Nichols, Screenplay: Nora Ephron & Alice Arlen, Producer: Michael Hausman. Meryl Streep (Karen Silkwood), Kurt Russell (Drew Stephens), Cher (Colly Pelliker), Craig T. Nelson (Winston).

Streep plays the real life Karen Silkwood who works in a plutonium factory. After being accidentally exposed to a lethal dose of radiation, she decides to blow the whistle on her employer, but before she can, she dies in mysterious circumstances.

Awards: Academy Award nominations, Best Actress: Meryl Streep. Golden Globes nominations, Best Actress in a Motion Picture: Meryl Streep.

131 mins. (ABC Motion Pictures)

In Our Hands (1984)

Director/Producer: Stan Warnow, Voice over: Meryl Streep & Anne Twomey.

A compilation documentary covering the huge anti-nuclear rally held in New York City on June 12th, 1982.

90 mins. (June 12 Film Goup & Libra-Cinema 5 Films)

Falling In Love (1984)

Director: Ulu Grosbard, Screenplay: Michael Cristofer, Producer: Marvin Worth. Meryl Streep (Molly Gilmore), Robert De Niro (Frank Raftis), Harvey Keitel (Ed Lasky), Jane Kaczmarek (Ann Raftis)

Meryl Streep and De Niro meet by chance in New York City and fall head-over-heels for each other; the only problem – they're both married.

106 mins. (Paramount Pictures)

Plenty (1985)

Director: Fred Schepisi, Screenplay: David Hare, Producer: Joseph Papp & Edward R. Pressman. Meryl Streep: (Susan Traherne), Charles Dance (Raymond Brock), Tracey Ullman (Alice Park), John Gielgud (Sir Leonard Darwin).

Meryl Streep plays a disillusioned woman looking for meaning at the end of World War II. After the excitement of being in the French Resistance, in peacetime she finds it hard to make her life live up to her expectations.

121 mins. (Pressman Productions & RKO Pictures)

Out Of Africa (1985)

Director: Sydney Pollack, Novel by: Karen Blixen, Biography by: Judith Thurman, Screenplay: Kurt Luedtke, Producer: Sydney Pollack. Meryl Streep (Karen Blixen), Robert Redford (Denys Finch Hatton), Klaus Maria Brandauer (Bror Blixen/Hans Blixen), Michael Kitchen (Berkley Cole).

Streep is the Danish Karen Blixen, who marries for the title of Baroness and starts a coffee plantation in Africa. Due to a disastrous marriage Karen begins an affair with Finch Hatton but she can't tame his free spirit.

Awards: Academy Award Nominations, Best Actress: Meryl Streep. Best Actress in a Motion Picture – Drama: Meryl Streep.

150 mins. (Universal Pictures)

Heartburn (1986)

Director: Mike Nichols, Novel by Nora Ephron, Screenplay: Nora Ephron, Producers: Robert Greenhut & Mike Nichols. Mery Streep (Rachel Samstat), Jack Nicholson (Mark Forman), Jeff Daniels (Richard), Maureen Stapleton (Vera).

Based on Nora Epron's autobiographical novel, Streep sports a black wig to play a food writer who tries to hold her marriage together despite her husband's philandering ways.

108 mins. (Paramount Pictures)

Ironweed (1987)

Director: Hector Babenco, Novel by: William Kennedy, Screenplay: William Kennedy, Producer: Keith Barish. Meryl Streep (Helen Archer), Jack Nicholson (Francis Phelan), Carroll Baker (Annie Phelan), Michael O'Keefe (Billy Phelan)

It's Halloween during the Great Depression. Alcoholic ex-radio singer Helen Archer (Streep) and ex-baseball pitcher Francis

Phelan (Nicholson) are a longtime couple doing their best to make it through each day using drink and memories.

Awards: Academy Award nominations, Best Actress: Meryl Streep.

143 mins. (HBO)

A Cry In the Dark/Evil Angels (1988)

Director: Fred Schepisi, Novel by: John Bryson, Screenplay: Robert Caswell & Fred Schepisi, Producer: Verity Lambert. Meryl Streep (Lindy Chamberlain) Sam Neill (Michael Chamberlain).

Streep plays real-life Lindy Chamberlain whose baby was killed by a dingo. But the public hue and cry, fuelled by the press and false forensic evidence, lead the police to put her on trial and she is imprisoned for a crime which she did not commit.

Awards: Academy Awards nominations, Best Actress: Meryl Streep. Best Actress in a Motion Picture – Drama: Meryl Streep.

120 min. (Canon Entertainment & Cinema Verity)

She-Devil (1989)

Director: Susan Seidelman, Novel by: Fay Weldon, Screenplay: Barry Strugatz & Mark R. Burns, Producer: Jonathan Brett & Susan Seidelman. Meryl Streep (Mary Fisher), Roseanne Barr (Ruth Patchett), Ed Begley Jr. (Bob), Linda Hunt (Hooper).

In this comedy adaptation of 'The Life and Loves of a She-Devil' Streep plays a spoiled Romantic novelist who steals Roseanne's husband away. Roseanne sets out on a path of revenge.

Awards: Golden Globe nominations, Best Actress in a Motion Picture – Comedy/Musical: Meryl Streep.

99 mins. (Orion Pictures)

Postcards From The Edge (1990)

Director: Mike Nichols, Novel by: Carrie Fisher, Screenplay: Carrie Fisher, Producers: John Calley & Mike Nichols. Meryl Streep (Suzanne Vale), Shirley MacLaine (Doris Mann), Dennis Quaid (Jack Faulkner), Gene Hackman (Lowell Kolcheck).

Streep plays druggie actress Suzanne Vale in Fisher's biopic comedy of her relationship with her mother, Debbie Reynolds

Awards: Academy Award nominations, Best Actress: Meryl Streep. Best Actress in a Motion Picture – Comedy/Musical: Meryl Streep.

101 mins. (Columbia Pictures)

Defending Your Life (1991)

Director: Albert Brooks, Screenplay: Albert Brooks, Producer: Michael Grillo. Meryl Streep (Julia), Albert Brooks (Daniel Miller), Rip Torn (Bob Diamond), Lee Grant (Lena Foster).

Albert Brooks plays Daniel Miller, a man who has everything until he crashes his BMW, sending his soul to Judgement City where he must show he's lived a good life. In this land of limbo he meets the woman of his dreams in Julia (Streep).

112 mins. (Geffen Pictures)

Death Becomes Her (1992)

Director: Robert Zemeckis, Screenplay by: Martin Donovan and David Koepp, Producers: Steve Starkey & Robert Zemeckis. Meryl Streep (Madeline Ashton), Bruce Willis (Dr Ernest Menville), Goldie Hawn (Helen Sharp), Isabella Rossellini (Lisle von Rhoman).

Streep, an actress, and Hawn, a writer, are ex-bestfriends who go toe to toe over beauty and plastic surgeon Bruce Willis in

226

this fantasy black comedy about the need to remain looking young, no matter what the cost.

Awards: Golden Globe nominations, Best Actress In a Motion Picture – Comedy/Musical: Meryl Streep.

104 mins. (Universal Pictures)

The House Of The Spirits (1993)

Director: Bille August, Novel by: Isabel Allende, Screenplay: Bille August, Producer: Bernd Eichinger. Meryl Streep (Clara del Valle Trueba), Glenn Close (Ferula Trueba), Jeremy Irons (Esteban Trueba), Winona Ryder (Blanca Trueba).

Streep plays the clairvoyant mother in the story of the trials and tribulations of three generations of a Chilean family. An adaptation of Isabelle's Allende's magical-fantasy novel.

140 mins. (Costa do Castelo Filmes, Det Danske Filminstitut, Eurimages, Neue Constantin Film & Spring Creek Productions)

The River Wild (1994)

Director: Curtis Hanson, Screenplay: Denis O'Neill, Producer: David Foster & Lawrence Turman. Meryl Streep (Gail Hartman), Kevin Bacon (Wade), David Strathairn (Tom), John C. Riley (Terry).

Streep plays a whitewater rafting guide who takes her family on a river trip. The trip turns into a nightmare when they offer to help two apparently stranded men who turn out be desperate criminals on the run from the police following a robbery.

Awards: Golden Globes nominations, Best Actress in a Motion Picture: Meryl Streep.

108 mins. (Universal Pictures)

The Simpsons (1994)

Creator: Matt Groening, Director: Susie Dietter. Meryl Streep (Jessica Lovejoy), Dan Castellaneta (Homer Simpson), Julie Kavner (Marge Simpson), Nancy Cartwright (Bart Simpson).

Streep voices Bart Simpson's girlfriend, the manipulative Jessica Lovejoy, who steals from the collection plate in church and puts the blame on him.

22mins. (Gracie Films, 20th Century Fox Televison & Film Roman Productions)

The Bridges Of Madison County (1995)

Director: Clint Eastwood, Novel By: Robert James Waller. Screenplay: Richard LaGravenese, Producers: Clint Eastwood & Kathleen Kennedy. Meryl Streep (Francesca Johnson), Clint Eastwood (Robert Kincaid), Annie Corley (Carolyn Johnson), Victor Slezak (Michael Johnson).

Set in 1965 Iowa, Streep plays a middle-aged housewife, bored with her life until romance comes literally knocking on her door in the form of Clint Eastwood. He is a National Geographic photographer on assignment to photograph the bridges of Madison County.

Awards: Academy Awards nominated, Best Actress: Meryl Streep. Golden Globes nominated, Best Actress in a Motion Picture – Drama: Meryl Streep.

135 mins. (Amblin Entertainment, Malpaso Productions & Warner Bros.)

Before and After (1996)

Director: Barbet Schroder, Novel by: Rosellen Brown, Screenplay by Ted Tally, Producer: Susan Hoffman. Meryl Streep (Dr Carolyn

Ryan), Liam Neeson (Ben Ryan), Edward Furlong (Jacob Ryan), Julia Weldon (Judith Ryan).

When their son is accused of murdering his girlfriend, his parents, Streep and Neeson, seek to prove his innocence whilst trying to hold their family together.

108 mins. (Caravan Pictures & Hollywood Pictures)

Marvin's Room (1996)

Director: Jerry Zaks, Screenplay: Scott McPherson, Producers: Robert De Niro, Scott Rudin & Jane Rosenthal. Meryl Streep (Lee), Leonardo DiCaprio (Hank), Diane Keaton (Bessie), Robert De Niro (Dr Wally).

Streep plays the estranged sister of Diane Keaton and mother of pyromaniac Leonardo DiCaprio. Keaton comes looking for Streep when she's diagnosed with cancer and needs a bone marrow transplant from a close relative.

Awards: Golden Globe nominations, Best Actress in a Motion Picture – Drama: Meryl Streep.

98 mins. (Scott Rudin Productions & Tribeca Productions)

Dancing At Lughnasa (1998)

Director: Pat O'Connor, Play by: Brian Friel, Screenplay by: Frank McGuiness, Producer: Noel Pearson. Meryl Streep (Kate 'Kit' Mundy), Michael Gambon (Father Jack Mundy), Catherine McCormack (Christina 'Chrissy' Mundy), Kathy Burke (Margaret 'Maggie' Mundy).

In 1936 on a Donegal Farm, Streep plays the eldest of five unmarried sisters struggling to make ends meet.

95 mins. (Bord Scannan na Eireann, Capitol Films, Channel Four Films, Ferndale Films, Radio Telefis Eireann & Sony Picture Classics)

One True Thing (1998)

Director: Carl Franklin, Novel by: Anna Quindlen, Screenplay by: Karen Croner, Producers: Jesse Beaton & Harry J. Ufland. Meryl Streep (Kate Gulden), Renee Zellweger (Ellen Gulden), William Hurt (George Gulden), Tom Everett Scott (Brian Gulden).

Renee Zellweger plays a career minded New York writer who returns to the family home to tend to her mother, Streep, who has been struck down by cancer.

Awards: Academy Awards nominations, Best Actress: Meryl Streep. Golden Globe nominations, Best Actress in a Motion Picture – Drama: Meryl Streep.

127 mins. (Monarch Pictures, Ufland & Universal Pictures)

Music of the Heart (1999)

Director: Wes Craven, Screenplay: Pamela Gray, Producers: Susan Kaplan, Marianne Maddalena & Allan Miller. Meryl Streep (Roberta Guaspari), Cloris Leachman (Assunta Guaspari), Aidan Quinn (Brian Turner), Angela Bassett (Principal Janet Williams).

In this true story Streep plays a violin teacher who fights against the New York Education Board to teach the violin to Harlem inner-city kids. She succeeds so well that her young students play at the world famous Carnegie Hall.

Awards: Academy Award nominations, Best Actress: Meryl Streep, Golden Globe nominations, Best Actress in a Motion Picture – Drama: Meryl Streep.

124 mins. (Miramax Films)

Adaptation (2002)

Director: Spike Jonze, Novel by: Susan Orlean, Screenplay by: Charlie Kaufman, Producers: Jonathan Demme, Vincent Landay & Edward Saxon. Meryl Streep (Susan Orlean), Nicholas Cage (Charlie/Donald Kaufman), Chris Cooper (John Laroche), Tilda Swinton (Valerie Thomas).

Streep plays a non-fiction writer whose book 'The Orchid Thief' is being adapted by Nicholas Cage, a gifted but neurotic screenwriter. Finding the process very difficult the writer ends up putting himself into the screenplay and falling in love with Streep (Orlean) while she ends up having an affair with the subject of her book, the orchid thief himself, John Laroche.

Awards: Golden Globes won, Best Actress in a Supporting Role in a Motion Picture: Meryl Streep.

114 mins. (Beverly Detroit, Clinica Estetico, Good Machine, Intermedia, Magnet Productions & Propaganda Films)

The Hours (2002)

Director: Stephen Daldry, Novel by: Michael Cunningham, Screenplay by: David Hare, Producers: Robert Fox & Scott Rudin. Meryl Streep (Clarissa Vaughan), Nicole Kidman (Virginia Woolf), Julianne Moore (Laura Brown), Stephen Dillane (Leonard Woolf).

In this adaptation from the play by Michael Cunningham set in three different eras, an almost unrecognizable Nicole Kidman, in a prosthetic nose, plays Virginia Woolf who's trying to start her book 'Mrs Dalloway'. In 1950s California Julianne Moore reads 'Mrs Dalloway' and prepares for a birthday party for her husband whom she doesn't love. Streep plays a Manhattan publisher, a lesbian who's struggling to prepare a party for her ex-husband, an esteemed author dying of aids.

Awards: Golden Globe nominations, Best Actress in a Motion Picture – Drama: Meryl Streep.

144 mins. (Paramount Pictures & Miramax Films)

Angels in America (2003)

Director: Mike Nichols, Screenplay (from his own play): Tony Kushner, Producer Celia D. Costas. Al Pacino (Roy Cohn), Meryl Streep (Hannah Pitt/Ethel Rosenberg/Rabbi/Angel of Australia), Emma Thompson (Nurse Emily/Homeless Woman/Angel of America), Jeffrey Wright (Belize/Mr Lies/Angel of Europe), Justin Kirk (Prior Walter/Leatherman in Park).

Tony Kushner's television adaptation of his Pulitzer Prize-winning stage play about the plight of those stricken by AISs in an indifferent America and the failure of the 'melting pot' society.

Awards: Emmies, Outstanding Lead Actress in a Mini-series or a Movie: Meryl Streep.

352 mins. (HBO)

'Freedom: A History of Us' (2003)

Writer: Philip Kunhardt Jr. Meryl Streep (Abigail Adams) – 4 Episodes,

A 16 episode serialization of the History of America with actors reading their roles.

(Public Broadcasting Service)

The Manchurian Candidate (2004)

Director: Jonathan Demme, Novel by: Richard Condon. Screenplay: George Axelrod (1962), Daniel Pyne, Dean Georgaris. Producers: Jonathan Demme, Ilona Herzberg, Scott Rudin, Tina Sinatra. Denzel Washington (Capt. Bennett Marco), Sgt. Raymond Shaw (Liev Schreiber), Senator Eleanor Shaw (Meryl Streep)

In this remake of Richard Condon's 1962 political thriller, Capt. Bennett Marco (Denzel Washington) and Sgt. Raymond Shaw (Liev Schreiber) are taken captive during the first Gulf War and brainwashed. Streep plays the manipulative, ice-cube chewing

Senator Eleanor Shaw who, ten years later, is party to the Manchurian Global Corporation's attempt to put their puppet and her son, Raymond, into the White House.

Awards: Golden Globes nominated. Best Actress in a Motion Picture – Drama: Meryl Streep.

Lemony Snicket's A Series Of Unfortunate Events
(2004)

Director: Brad Silberling, Books: Daniel Handler, Screenplay: Robert Gordon, Producers: Laurie MacDonald, Walter F. Parkes & Jim Van Wyck. Jim Carrey (Count Olaf), Meryl Streep (Aunt Josephine), Liam Aiken (Klaus), Emily Browning (Violet).

A group of child siblings are left in the care of the eccentric Count Olaf after their parents perish in a house fire. Unable to get their inherited fortune until they're adults, the children are at the mercy of greedy Olaf. Streep plays their aunt who is afraid of everything but does have the childrens' best interests at heart.

108 mins. (Paramount Pictures, DreamWorks SKG & Scott Rudin Productions))

Prime (2005)

Director: Ben Younger, Screenplay: Ben Younger, Producers: Jennifer Todd & Suzanne Todd. Meryl Streep (Lisa Metzger), Uma Thurman (Rafi Gardet), Bryan Greenberg (David Bloomberg), Jon Abrahams (Morris).

Streep is an analyst who's helping Uma Thurman get over her recent messy divorce. When Thurman meets a 23-year-old painter and begins a relationship, Streep encourages her and tells Thurman to forget the age difference and go for it – until she finds out it's her own son.

105 mins. (Universal Pictures)

A Prairie Home Companion (2006)

Director: Robert Altman, Screenplay: Garrison Keillor, Producers: Robert Altman, Wren Arthur, Joshua Astrachan, Tony Judge & David Levy. Meryl Streep (Yolanda Johnson) Woody Harrelson (Dusty), Tommy Lee Jones (The Axeman), Garrison Keillor (GK).

Garrison Keillor's long running radio show of the same name is put onto celluloid in the shape of a comedy musical about its last ever broadcast. Streep and Lily Tomlin play the singing Johnson Sisters, Lindsay Lohan is Streep's suicide-obsessed singing daughter and Tommy Lee Jones plays the axe man sent to close down the radio show.

105 min. (Picturehouse Entertainment, Greenestreet Films, River Road Entertainment, Sandcastle 5 Productions & Armenia Film Studios.)

The Music of Regret (2006)

Director: Laurie Simmons, Screenplay: Laurie Simmons & Matthew Weinstein, Producers: Don Faller and Laurie Simmons. Meryl Streep (The Woman) Adam Gue (The Man – voice), Tony Nation (Ted – voice), John Tully (Tod – voice).

Streep agreed to star in artist Laurie Simmons's first short film, a musical that reflects on her own childhood.

40 mins. (Double Wide Media, Performa & Salon 94)

The Devil Wears Prada (2006)

Director: David Frankel, Novel by Lauren Weisberger, Screenplay: Aline Brosh McKenna, Producer: Wendy Finerman. Meryl Streep (Miranda Priestly), Anne Hathaway(Andrea Sachs), Emily Blunt (Emily), Stanley Tucci (Nigel).

Streep plays the over-the-top, fearsome fashion magazine editor of Runway (Weisberger, who wrote the original novel, was an

234

assistant to Anna Wintour on Vogue). Anne Hathaway is her hapless new assistant who has to go through an ordeal of fire to prove herself.

Awards: Academy Award nominations, Best Actress: Meryl Streep. Golden Globes, Best Actress in a Motion Picture: Meryl Streep.

109 mins. (Fox 2000)

Dark Matter (2007)

Director: Shi-Zeng Chen, Screenplay: Billy Shebar, Producer: Andrea Miller, Mary Salter & Janet Yang. Meryl Streep (Joanna Silver), Liu Xing (Ye Liu), Aidan Quinn (Reiser).

Loosely based on a real events, Streep plays a university patron who befriends and naively prompts Liu Xing, a Ph.D. physics student from China, to clash with his professor over their opposing theses. After becoming alienated by a sucession of let downs, Liu Xing goes on a shooting spree.

90 mins. (Saltmill & Myriad Pictures)

Evening (2007)

Director: Lajos Koltai, Novel by: Susan Minot, Screenplay by: Susan Minot & Michael Cunningham, Producer: Jeff Sharp. Meryl Streep (Lila Ross) Claire Danes (Ann Grant), Toni Colette (Nina Mars), Vanessa Redgrave (Ann Lord).

Gathered round their mother's (Vanessa Redgrave) deathbed, two daughters (Claire Danes and Toni Colette) discover their mother had always been in love with someone she met 50 years before at her best friend's high society wedding. We flashback to the wedding and see the young lovers meet. For the first time Streep appeared in a film with her daughter, Mamie Gummer.

117 mins. (Focus features, Hart-Sharp Entertainment, MBF Erste Filmproduktiongesellschaft & Twins Financing)

Lions For Lambs (2007)

Director: Robert Redford, Screenplay: Matthew Michael Carnahan, Producers: Matthew Michael Carnahan, Tracy Falco, Andrew Hauptman & Robert Redford. Meryl Streep (Janine Roth), Robert Redford (Professor Stephen Malley), Tom Cruise (Senator Jasper Irving), Michael Pena (Ernest Rodriguez).

Three stories are told in simultaneous real time. The tale of two college students who decide to fight in Iraq. A republican senator (Tom Cruise) on the rise is interviewed by a shrewd journalist (Streep) about the government's exit strategy in Iraq. Redford is a college professor who tries to re-engage a gifted but disenchanted student back into his class.

92 mins. (United Artists, Cruise/Wagner Productions, & Wildwood Enterprises)

Rendition (2008)

Director: Gavin Hood, Screenplay by: Kelley Sane, Producer: Steve Golin & Marcus Viscidi. Meryl Streep (Corrie Whitman), Jake Gyllenhaal (Douglas Freeman), Reese Witherspoon (Isabella Fields El-Ibrahimi), Omar Metwally (Anwar El-Ibrahimi).

'Extraordinary Rendition' is the process whereby terrorist suspects can be delivered to countries who routinely use torture to obtain information. Streep plays the unbending senior official who authorizes the kidnap and interrogation of Omar Metwally, husband of Reese Witherspoon, who is pregnant and desperate to find him.

122 mins. (New Line Cinema)

Mamma Mia! (2008)

Director: Phyllida Lloyd, Screenplay: Catherine Johnson, Producers: Judy Craymer & Gary Goetzman. Meryl Streep (Donna Sheridan), Pierce Brosnan (Sam Carmichael), Colin Firth (Harry Bright), Stellan Skarsgard (Bill Anderson).

The hit film of the successful stage musical. Streep is a dungareed mother who runs a hotel on a small Greek Island. When her daughter decides to get married, she discovers her mother's old diary which records her love life and invites three men, one of whom must be her father, to her wedding without her mother's knowledge. The story is set to ABBA songs.

Awards: (2009): Golden Globes nominations, Best Actress in a Motion Picture – Musical/Comedy: Meryl Streep.

108 mins. (Universal Pictures)

Doubt (2008)

Director: John Patrick Shanley, Screenplay: John Patrick Shanley, Producer: Scott Rudin. Meryl Streep (Sister Aloysius Beauvier), Philip Seymour Hoffman (Father Brendan Flynn), Amy Adams (Sister James), Viola Davis (Mrs Miller).

In 1964, Principal Sister Aloysius runs St Nicholas church school, with a rod of iron believing in the power of fear and discipline to keep order. When a younger Sister, Amy Adams, vents her concern that Father Flynn (Philip Seymour Hoffman) is paying too much attention to a particular student, Sister Aloysius persecutes the Father without any proof.

Awards: (2009): Golden Globe Nominations, Best Actress in a Motion Picture: Meryl Streep.

104 mins. (Scott Rudin Productions for Miramax Films.)

Bibliography

Diana Maychick (1985), *Meryl Streep, the Reluctant Superstar*. St Martin's Press.

Eugene Pfaff Jr and Mark Emerson (1987), *Meryl Streep – A Critical Biography*; McFarland and Co.

Acknowledgements

Copy editor: Michael Carson

Picture Research: Josine Meijer

Publicity: Melissa O'Young

Picture Credits

Courtesy of Yale Drama School: Plates 1, 2.

Courtesy of the author: Plate 6 bottom

Courtesy of Corbis: Plate 6 top, Plate 12 top

Courtesy of Getty Images: Plate 5 (top) (Tom Wargacki/ WireImage), Plate 16

Courtesy of Kobal Collection:
    Front Cover (Universal Playtone)
    Plate 3 top (EMI/Columbia/Warners)
    Plate 4 (United Artists/Brian Hamill)
    Plate 7 (United Artists)
    Plate 8 (Columbia)
    Plates 9, 10 top (Universal)
    Plate 10 bottom (Amblin/Malpaso/Ken Regan)
    Plate 12 bottom (Miramax/Andrew Schwartz)
    Plate 13 (20th Century Fox/Brigitte Lacombe)
    Plates 14, 15 (Universal/Playtone)

Courtesy of PA Photos: Plate 11

Courtesy of 20th Century Fox: Plate 13

239

The publisher would like to thank Ray Buckland and Keyboard Services for their assiduous typesetting – and, also, Martin Hay.